THE LAST FISHERMAN

*Witness to the
Endangered Oceans*

JEFFREY L. ROTMAN

WITH **YAIR HAREL**

INTRODUCTION BY **LES KAUFMAN**

ABBEVILLE PRESS
NEW YORK LONDON

Australian spearfishing champion with a prize dogtooth tuna caught 200 miles off the eastern coast of Australia. (page 1)

Southern stingrays, Grand Cayman Island, Caribbean (pages 2–3)

Dana Rotman, the photographer's daughter, with a bottlenose dolphin at Dolphin Reef, Eilat, Israel. (page 5)

Duritara, **a fishing boat** used for turtle hunting in Miskito Cays in the Caribbean waters. (pages 6–7)

Mario Orlando on the *Padre Pio* 20 miles off the coast of Gloucester, Mass. Yellowtail flounder are caught in a net. (front cover)

Tomato clownfish and sea anemone, Sipadan Island, Borneo (back cover)

Editor: Joan Strasbaugh
Text editor: Carrie Bebris
Designer: Patricia Fabricant
Production manager: Louise Kurtz

All photographs are by Jeffrey L. Rotman unless noted otherwise.
Photo on page 30 by Ken Beck. Photo on page 43 by Isabelle Delafosse.

First edition
10 9 8 7 6 5 4 3 2 1

Library of Congress Cataloging-in-Publication Data

Rotman, Jeffrey L.
  The last fisherman : witness to the endangered oceans / by Jeffrey L. Rotman and Yair Harel ; introduction by Les Kaufman. — First edition.
     pages cm
  Includes bibliographical references and index.
  ISBN 978-0-7892-1191-0 (hardcover : alk. paper) 1. Underwater photography. 2. Marine photography. 3. Saltwater fishing—Pictorial works. 4. Overfishing. 5. Rotman, Jeffrey L.—Travel. I. Harel, Yair. II. Title.
  TR800.R666 2014
  778.7'3—dc23
                        2014016848

For bulk and premium sales and for text adoption procedures, write to Customer Service Manager, Abbeville Press, 137 Varick Street, New York, NY 10013, or call 1-800-ARTBOOK.

Visit Abbeville Press online at www.abbeville.com.

FOR MY BOYS: ITAMAR, OMRI, AND IDO
—YAIR HAREL

FOR MY KIDS: ADAM, DANA, MATTHEW, AND THOMAS
—JEFFREY ROTMAN

CONTENTS

INTRODUCTION
A SPACE
TO HEAL

BY LES KAUFMAN

When the layout came for this book, my first reaction was to reflexively check the pictures for misidentifications, chapter after chapter. As I reached the end, though, I realized that Jeff Rotman and Yair Harel have done a remarkable thing. For years I'd been trying to wake people up to the crazy things they are doing to the ocean, by accident and by design. My colleagues and I have shown data, graphs, statistics, history, genetic and isotopic analyses, and reams of peer-reviewed, published literature. We held our noses and went out to prove and prove again the obvious—that humanity is eating, dredging, poisoning, souring, and boiling its way through two thirds of our planet, draining what we once thought limitless, changing what we'd once thought immutable.

Our efforts have been largely to no avail.

Here, instead, Jeff and Yair have captured the arc of a lifetime on and under the sea: what it's like to live between the tides and to witness monumental change. Looking forward to each day with the sea, we anticipate its fecund richness and kaleidoscopic wonders. Looking back across decades, however, the authors see an ocean experiencing an abrupt and sweeping upheaval. The signs are there, but these are merely the symptoms, the ripple effects of changes deeper yet. Incredibly we have pulled the plug on the ocean and watched as its wealth first circled, then vanished down the drain of insatiable opportunism. Now we stand staring down the hole, in a state of shock, wondering what can be done.

As you glide through the authors' adventures, you will see what they've seen, feel what they've felt, and arrive at a depth of understanding you could not have reached via any amount of numerical data. Sometimes the "data" it takes to open our eyes and minds are raw and emotional, gut-punching images and words; a salty, wet passion play.

I have witnessed firsthand what Jeff and Yair have brought you on these pages. A fisherman by avocation, my work as a marine biologist brings me eye to eye with some of the same individual fishes that I might catch and eat. I think and worry about species, but it is individual pairs of eyes that watch me as I lift a net or jot numbers on my underwater slate. I am a hunter-killer and a doctor, in one contradictory package. Staring

Unknown to scientists at the time it was captured on film, this transparent creature found in the Red Sea has since been identified as a deep-sea pelagic eel. The purpose of its circular pose remains a mystery as does the smaller creature within.

into the eyes of my quarry—whether I hunt this day to fill a table with food, or a table with data—always makes me uncomfortable . . . as it has unsettled all hunters since the dawn of humanity. My station in life is comparable to that of the authors: more years behind than ahead, a short, colorful thread in the fabric of life in a sacred place and an ancient role. I am gladdened to join this book's authors and our legions of compatriots who rise in darkness to "go down to the sea." If you ask a bunch of them to comment on what I've said here, they'd likely roll their eyes and get back to work; if your line isn't in the water you're not going to catch anything.

Fishermen (including women; the term is gender-neutral) are acutely aware of the fabric of which they are a part. Whatever their local heritage, fishermen share the transcendent Eastern view of the world as an interconnected web, an emergent whole that cannot be fully fathomed or anticipated, though we must try to do so every day to make our bread. Western science is just edging toward a full embrace of this reality; fishermen have been living it for ages. The fisherman trusts his or her ability to read the water, to think like a fish, to navigate a richly veined and varied living world that to the landlubber looks a dead and trackless gunmetal gray. The fisherman feels a mystical part of this enormous wholeness, knowing always that one slip, one carelessness or meaningless accident, can abruptly cut short his or her thread of existence. The fisherman is hunted, and haunted, by chance.

The numbers of fishermen, as the numbers of people on earth, has swelled alarmingly in recent years. We saw it coming, and still allowed this to happen. The fishes have failed to follow suit: In a merciless calculus, the more of us the fewer of them.

Our human genius has touched the waters and made them as clear as glass to our sophisticated electronics and powerful floating death machines. It isn't as if others haven't noticed, and now the fisherman is under siege—to many, the villain of this story. How foolish can you be, killing the goose that lays your golden eggs? As any honest fisherman will admit (they're not so scarce as legend would suggest), were there one last fish in the world, he'd just as soon land it and let Hemingway's Old Man roll over in his watery grave. Fishermen are well aware that pursuit of their livelihood has brought the living ocean to its knees. Is it the fishermen's fault that there are now so few fish, and that they are so small? Yes, of course it is. At this moment. But it is not his or her fault—any more than yours or mine—that our entire life support system is frayed and weak, spraying pieces of itself into the void, and unraveling before our eyes. It is not the fisherman's fault that all of us live in the shadow of the sword. The fisherman knows that the world can and very well might go on without him any instant, an awareness that humanity as a whole is artfully dodging at its existential peril.

CARIBBEAN, MID-1970s TO MID-1980s

Bigfin reef squid caught in a gill net laid down on the coral reefs of the Red Sea by Bedouin fishermen.

Bill lifted the trap from the waters of Little Lameshur Bay in a single fluid motion. He peered through the crude wattle-and-wire structure at a pulsing pile of festively colored reef fishes. A few quick pokes with his sharp stick, and the noisiest among them were quiet. Every morning Bill hopped into his small skiff to tend his traps, bringing mostly small parrotfishes, doctor, grunts, and groupers back from the coral reef to feed his family and make a little money on the side. The rest of this month of June 1974, Bill was keeping me fed and out of trouble as I pursued my first field research outside the mainland United States, studying coral reefs in the Virgin Islands.

Bill and I weren't the only ones on the water. Hundreds of Virgin Islanders set out in little boats in the same way each day that hundreds of thousands of Caribbean men (mostly) had brought fish to their women century after century, up until today when nearly all the fishes were tiny and few just about everywhere we looked. Lush fields and stately forests of mustard-colored corals stretched over a gently rolling sea bottom spread beneath crystal, sunlit waters. All blue-on-blue serenity, but very few big animals; mostly

Sohal surgeonfish, Red Sea, Egypt
Caught in a net by local fishermen.

glimmering shoals of tiny mites like those now lying still in the bottom of Bill's boat. The sweet little hind—Bill called them "butterfish"—were a welcome break from spaghetti at every meal.

At the time we didn't think much about how small the fishes all were. We enjoyed the breeze and each other's company, failing utterly to see the darkness all along the horizon. In the wake of centuries of overfishing, the Caribbean was a ghost ship, carpeted with gorgeous, lush fields of coral, but drained of the hordes of fishes, lobster, sea turtles, manatee, and conch that had once dotted the reefs and mowed the meadows of seagrass at densities beyond belief.

Not ten years after my time with Bill came the Beginning of the End. Caribbean corals increasingly succumbed to sweeping plagues and a warming ocean. Seaweed-eating sea urchins also fell to an unknown pathogen, while the big seaweed-eating parrotfishes and surgeonfishes were long since reduced to the equivalent of herbivorous sardines. Absent significant grazers, the spaces left bare were swamped by seaweed, and the seaweed stuck. Since corals find it extremely difficult to recruit and grow in the presence of a kelp canopy, many coral reefs were transformed into what scientists call "fleshy algal pavements."

The decline of coral reefs was first and most striking in the Caribbean, but the situation swept swiftly across the planetary midrib to ring a global death knell for all the world oceans' richest and most colorful environment. Coral reefs have ceased their upward growth in a rising ocean. Corals bake and die in ever greater and longer summer doldrums. Reefs are battered with mounting violence and frequency by a new breed of superstorm. The broken corals find it increasingly difficult to grow and repair their skeletons in an acidifying sea. Most coral reefs today are tattered, mere suggestions of what a coral reef should be, yet affluent sport divers continue to throng to them, somehow missing that they've become mausoleums. Certainly, the tourist industry would rather they not notice, and does everything possible to quell the frantic smoke signals of island states and scientists to an unseeing world.

Meanwhile, land-based impacts surge along with human population, people busily denuding watersheds and spewing waste from seven billion fire hoses. The outcome is evident: an end to the current 10,000-year epoch of coral reef growth—an indelible mark in the fossil record of life on earth. Coral reefs could vanish within the lifetimes of those reading these words.

But that isn't the end of the story. Unprotected by living, growing coral reefs, beaches and shorelines will erode in the face of rising seas, draining away vibrant coastal economies with them. So will go the most desired living places, the sources of food and livelihood for the quarter of humanity that inhabits the warm coastal lowlands of our planet.

STELLWAGEN BANK, MASSACHUSETTS, MID-2000s

Though not much for 3AM rousings, I loved being out with Paul and his dad, Leo, on the *Angela and Rose*, dragging Stellwagen Bank, 30 miles off Boston, for cod, haddock, flounder and whatnot with a great big trawl. Our grant for cooperative research paid for the fuel, and we could bank our catch back into the research account to add days to our ledger. We were fishing in a no-trawling zone for good reason: Our mission was to see if the exclusion of trawlers for several years had actually resulted in the intended effect of helping to rebuild groundfish populations, nursery habitat for fishes, and feeding grounds to support healthy fish stocks.

Legitimacy and a big sign on both sides of the wheelhouse didn't keep us from getting strafed by U.S. Coast Guard planes and boarded by coast guard vessels, all guys just doing their jobs. They had this job to do—in between moments of protecting the security of the homeland—because cod were in the basement. After centuries fueling the bottomless European, and later North American, hunger for fish fillets, the seas off Massachusetts were empty enough to echo. It didn't always seem that way, though, even now. Any fishermen worth their salt could spot their gear on some place where the remaining fish congregated, making the experience of catching them seem as much as ever like winning the lottery. A rigged lottery, perhaps—I glanced back at the ultramodern echo sounder and GPS that, combined with Leo and Paul's incredible store of knowledge and skill, amounted to a veritable vacuum for seafood deliciousness. Neither did our permit diminish the sweet sinfulness of fishing with impunity where nobody else was allowed. However, there was hell to pay for each glorious day of literally playing hooky: six-hour chasers in the lab after a fifteen-hour day of getting to, out upon, and back from sea.

It was 2004, and looking like Gulf of Maine cod might stage a recovery yet. Under harsh regulatory restrictions on the number of days fishermen could head out in their boats, on where they could fish, and on the size of fish they could legally take, the storied Gloucester fishermen had suffered—Paul and Leo among them, along with all their colleagues from Maine to Provincetown. Now, finally, it just might pay off. Haddock had rebounded in response to the stringent catch controls, and so a cod bonanza should be just around the corner—or so those of us on the Science and Statistics Committee figured. Indeed, not just cod, but all the overfished stocks of the place where America began would soon see a stop to overfishing and a chance to rebound to their former glory.

Except that's not what happened. One year the professional stock assessment for Gulf of Maine cod indicated a robust recovery. The next time round, it looked like the same fish might be headed for listing under the U.S. Endangered Species Act. The atmosphere in the Science and Statistics Committee meeting was funereal. While we were debating our next recommendation to the New England Fishery Management Council (the governing body for fisheries in New England), an esteemed Canadian fisheries scientist on the committee silently emailed several of us with the creepy news that the data under discussion bore a haunting resemblance to what the Canadian Maritimes had seen just before the cataclysmic collapse of its Atlantic cod stocks. Worse yet, fishing gear can be only so selective, so incidental catches of cod and other depleted species set the practical limit on catches of other more abundant fishes to ensure that the "weak links" aren't broken by accident.

This situation isn't unique to New England—nearly all the world's fisheries are now fully or even over-exploited, harboring a profusion of weak links whose rupture could profoundly alter or bring down the entire system. The staunch commercial fishermen of New England are staring down the end of the road for a hallowed and ancient way of life. They're not alone. Recreational fishermen—a big chunk of America—have also noticed the diminishing catches and hear stories from their parents and grandparents about how it used to be. Stories they may not even believe, a phenomenon known as the "shifting baseline."

Meanwhile in Gloucester, fishing is giving way to waterfront condos and forcibly quaint boutiques. Gorton's of Gloucester, proud employer of hundreds in this historic fishing town (and many a Middle American's only tangible link to the ocean), now gets its fish from Alaska—though for how long, nobody knows. The disappearing boats of Gloucester's storied waterfront can no longer make catch, contract, or mortgage. The Town of Gloucester has vowed to fight back . . . but against what?

TONLE SAP, CAMBODIA, 2010s

In May 2013 I found myself balancing across the gunnels of two narrow "long-tailed" boats, far from land, on the placid waters of Cambodia's Tonle Sap (Great Lake) in the heart of the Khmer domain. I was raptly pawing through a fisherman's gillnet catch of tiny, multicolored freshwater fishes. Half a world and forty years from Bill and Little Lameshur Bay, and still at the same game.

On a shrimp dragger, Atlantic side of Costa Rica Fishermen dragging in the shallow nurseries where shrimp are more plentiful, using mosquito netting with mesh so small that almost nothing escapes.

This was something truly different, though: more than three hundred species of fishes, all caught by fishermen, all useful—and used in some way. The life drawn from these waters nourishes millions of Cambodian citizens who derive nearly two-thirds of their protein requirements from Tonle Sap fish. The profusion of vessels, gear, fishermen, and lakeside abodes is nearly as stunning as the diversity of the fishes their lives are built upon. Presiding over the north end of the lake is the ancient temple city of Angkor Wat. Those who have trekked its vast grounds have seen the long frieze depicting an old Hindu story, the "Churning of the Sea of Milk." In this enduring work of art many fish species, both real and fanciful, are depicted vividly enough that the real ones can be identified to species, as ichthyologist Tyson Roberts has in fact done.

The spectacular burst of biomass that emanates from this lake every year—as fish, rice, and a host of wildlife products—is fueled by monsoon floods that flow backwards from the Mekong River and up the Tonle Sap River, swelling it annually into Southeast Asia's largest lake. The flooded lake basin covers vast areas of bushland and forest for seven months of the year. This is time enough for that enormous quantity of vegetable biomass to decompose and enter the lake food web. The resulting detritus, along with a bumper crop of plankton fueled by nutrient-rich sediments from the Mekong and Tonle Sap basins from as far away as China, are all funneled into an astonishingly large mass of fish. As the flood subsides and the lake disgorges water and wealth back into the Mekong, varied nets are cast into and across the raging stream, literally straining the lake. The catch is dominated by silvery *trey riel*, "money fish," a group of small, closely related species that are sliced and fermented to produce a paste called prahoc, the basis of many distinctly Khmer dishes. The people doing the catching are ethnic Khmer, Vietnamese, and Cham—a polyglot society inhabiting the lake on floating houses and stilted villages. The sloshy cornucopia is also fodder for immense Mekong catfish and other piscian giants, profuse water birds, water snakes, fishing cats, and a host of other strange and wonderful wildlife.

Once, not terribly long ago, tigers, elephants, crocodiles, and bears roamed lush flooded and semi-dry tropical forests surrounding the lake. Now forests and game alike are gone, save for scattered gibbons in temple woodlands like those of Angkor. Giant catfish, giant barb, and giant ray have mostly been replaced by pipsqueak remnants—joke survivors, like tiny plastic dinosaurs. And the people, survivors all, bear the transgenerational scars of brutality and oppression. Half suffer signs of post-traumatic stress disorder from the Khmer Rouge years experienced by themselves or their parents, yet they carry themselves with dignity, generosity, and renewed hopes for the future.

The overfishing of Tonle Sap is only the beginning of the tale, however. China, choking on coal dust and air pollution, seeks clean energy in hydropower. Cambodia, Laos, Thailand, and Vietnam are hungry for electricity, too, as well as for the steady supplies of water needed for modern, irrigated, industrialized rice production—none of this monsoon stuff. And so come the dams, which block the migrations of all the fishes that nurse in Tonle Sap and seek dry season refuge in the deeps of the main stem Mekong River. If all the biggest are built as planned, prized species will go extinct, and the annual explosion of protein from the Tonle Sap will narrow to a trickle.

But the dams are not all. China sees wealth in its neighbors, and wants its cut, too. So tropical forests laden with precious "luxury" woods have been nearly annihilated, and along with them all of their marvelous wildlife and forest products. In their wake: wall-to-wall manioc and rubber fields, pouring starch and natural rubber into wavering markets.

One iconic species after another is vanishing from the scene. Siamese crocodile are down to the last hundred pairs in the wild, yet tens of thousands lie in crocodile farms. With fish now too dear to use all the time as crocodile food, the farmers have turned to the lake's bumper crop of snakes, foraged by the millions each year until now they, too, can no longer be fully relied upon. Deep in jungle rivers once lurked an abundance of dragonfish, *Scleropages formosus*, a magnificently beautiful large aquarium fish of ancient affinities, reputed to bring the owner excellent luck. Dragonfish have spawned a massive luxury market for special variants whose big silvery scales glow metallically in vibrant automobile shades, yet the wild ones, still in ferocious demand, are now down to their dregs in a few forest strongholds.

All the forest, all the rivers, all the wildlife—the natural spirits and providers of Cambodia—are threatened, fading phantoms before a sterile, short-term vision of industrial wealth.

RESURRECTING OUR OCEAN EDEN

There is a world of stories of this same sort—stories about disappearing fishes and desperate fishermen in East Africa, New Zealand, Brazil, Fiji, Kiribati. I have colleagues who speak similarly of the Arctic, the North Sea, Argentina, California. Were these messages from a faraway alien planet, we would conclude that its inhabitants were doomed. The stories speak not only of vanishing species and ways of life, but of ecosystem failure. The scarcity of any one life form is merely symptomatic of greater forces at work toward more ominous ends. In the strange debate over "whether" global climate change was really happening (strange because the evidence is unequivocal), there was an iconic graph, the famous "hockey stick" popularized by Vice President Al Gore. That there has been a sweeping depletion of the world's fish stocks is equally difficult to challenge. Its signature might be called the "sliding pond," the trace of one stock decline after another—what scientists term "serial depletion." Until quite recently, everywhere that people have looked, the mark of overkill—like a mark of Zorro—lay there: easy to deny, but hard to miss.

In the United States the signs were at last observed and discussed, and a law was enacted to launch the rebuilding of exploited fish populations: the Fishery Conservation and Management Act of 1976. Sponsored by Senators Warren G. Magnuson of Washington State and Ted Stevens of Alaska, the law stipulated the use of "best available science" to set upper bounds on the intensity with which each species could be pursued. The act (now known as the "Magnuson-Stevens Act") has been updated and amended in an ongoing process for both the science and fishermen, as circumstances are ever-evolving.

At the time the act was passed, fisheries management focused on individual species or stocks. These were (and still are) understood in terms of a branch of ecology called "population biology," the same science used to understand the growth of the human population. Basically the idea was to figure out how many fish there would be next year, and then deliberately avoid catching all of them so some are around to repopulate for the coming years. When fish are very few, the population grows slowly because it takes a while for babies to survive and accumulate. When fish are very many, the population grows slowly because they're competing for food. So populations grow fastest right at the midway point in their growth curves, a reference point called "maximum sustainable yield" (MSY). Take just enough fish to leave the population at MSY, and it will bounce back as quickly as possible.

This is the theory on which most fishery laws are based. It may seem a ridiculously simplistic way to run things, but when there aren't too many people, fish species, or conflicting issues involved and people actually play by the rules, it isn't such a bad way of doing business. It all rests on rather shaky assumptions (fish are born and die at a constant rate, the ecosystem is in some kind of unshakeable equilibrium, species do not interact with each other much), but we make lots of decisions in an atmosphere of simplifying assumptions—in an "all else being equal" kind of way—just as a practical matter. As long as these decisions aren't life-and-death, things generally work out fine and when they don't, it isn't the end of the world. But what if we pushed the envelope to the breaking point? Then, a wrong decision would prove disastrous.

Well, for fisheries, we *have* pushed the envelope to the breaking point. We have overfished the entire world. Now, when we talk about letting a fish stock rebuild itself, we've forgotten how good it can be, and so we set our goals for what defines a healthy, fishable stock absurdly low. As long as we live on the edge, we are vulnerable to mistakes and unexpected changes in the nature of things. Two in particular come to mind. One is this dicey assumption that what you do to one species will not affect others that you are also concerned about. The reality is, as we all well know, that everything is connected to everything else. The second problem is harder to help, because it's in our wiring. Our thought process follows straight lines, but the world and the way things happen in it are psychedelically curvy and full of surprises.

Marine ecologists, of which fishery scientists are one specialization, have begun to come to grips with these two challenges: connectivity and nonlinearity—and what we're learning is really, really exciting.

Take connectivity. There is an obvious link between the global fishery crisis and the failure of fishery science to fully embrace the biological and economic interconnectedness of the *real* real world. There is no such thing as an isolated fish stock. Fishes of every species are embedded in the same ecosystem matrix that holds us all as grateful prisoners in the paper-thin biosphere that envelops our little rock. It isn't just about the ocean. The natural unit of ecosystem function that people occupy is not the town, or nation, or continent. It is a watershed and coastal ocean system. There are several related traditional management systems in Oceania that are set up on this basis, recognizing that what people do to trees on the ridges impacts their ability to fish on the reefs. The idea is so deeply rooted in how people think about themselves and who they are that being from a particular valley or watershed ecosystem—in Fiji this is called a *vanua*—supersedes the town or village for pride of place in one's personal universe. A vanua is just a discernibly self-contained chunk of the biosphere, a unit out of many such that fitted together form the planet's living landscape.

The idea of framing each decision about resource use in the context of the whole vanua has a Western counterpart, called "Ecosystem-Based Management" (EBM). EBM can be pursued in a very simple way by just placing everything that folks in a coastal region would like to do on the same map, and noting potential overlaps or conflicts. You can expect that things might work out better if compromises are found in advance of instituting any new policies. This "compatibility analysis" then enters the folio of stuff to

The *mattanza*, an ancient Sicilian method of bluefin tuna fishing, is disappearing from Mediterranean waters along with the fish it traditionally targets.

consider when decisions are being made. Of course, the process is made much easier by using computerized Geographic Information Systems (GIS) to compile and visualize all the relevant maps and data.

Usually people want to see possible outcomes in dollars and cents, not just in terms of intuitive (or even obvious) conflicts and cultural values. The things people need and want from nature are called *ecosystem services*—the flows of good stuff from nature to us, and wastes from us to nature for reprocessing. Our lives depend upon ecosystem services; they are not luxury items. Ecosystem services arise in a complicated way from patterns of land and ocean use, weather and climate, population density, and landscape history. Also, when people do things to maximize one ecosystem service, such as nature's ability to generate and provide access to herring to be caught in a fishery, it is often at the expense of other ecosystem services. In the case of herring, those taken (in huge numbers) for protein and vitamin supplements or for animal feed are literally being taken out of the mouths of whales (impacting whale-watching, a form of ecotourism), seabirds (often protected by national laws), endangered species (whale and seabirds both commonly among them), and even other fisheries such as cod, salmon, or tuna, fisheries whose health depends upon herring being available as forage. This is called an "ecosystem service tradeoff." It's all complicated enough, that here, again, a computer can be helpful. So we now have GIS-driven computer tools that help in understanding not only the nature and spatial extent of resource conflicts, but also the impact of any particular decision on the flows of dollars, cultural values, and quality-of-life experiences to various stakeholders.

The ability to manipulate maps and values on the computer is very helpful, but it's about today, not tomorrow; it of course doesn't warn you about unanticipated consequences or surprises in system dynamics. To see these, you have to understand all of the connections that bind fish and fowl, people and plankton, into the monolithic tapestry of life. You need a mathematical model that embraces complexity and its puzzling stepchild: what scientists refer to as "nonlinear" dynamics. Ecosystems and human societies—and most especially the two together—are archetypical complex systems. They can be stable (seemingly in balance at equilibrium) one minute, and then suddenly fly off to another very different sort of balance. If you're deeply invested in the first balance (in which perhaps cod are very abundant, but sea scallops are rare), the shift to another, different one may not be welcome (few cod, lots of scallops—as right now in New England). So we'd like to be able to predict such shifts, remembering that the reason they happen is because all things are connected in very complex ways. This requires a new math. One example of such a new math—a particularly useful one—is "nonlinear time series analysis," whose development has been led by Professor George Sugihara of Scripps University.

The melding of ecosystem service tradeoff models, nonlinear time series analysis and other exciting new tools are examples of how science has risen to the challenge of Ecosystem Based Management. Unfortunately, we scientists are not doing well in getting a rise out of many of the politicians and managers who are the actual deciders. They regard this new science as too new, too untested, and too complicated and hard to understand for them to be willing to put their trust in it. There is a deep irony here, and it's that the old science that they think they *do* understand is simply not up to the needs of a densely networked society on a planet undergoing rapid climate change. Of course, climate change isn't a problem at this moment if you choose to abandon science altogether and simply not believe in it, as too many people have chosen to do. Fishermen know better. Their lives are in the grip of the weather every day, and the climate over the course of their lives. They know when things are changing.

And things *are* changing. The science of EBM is being grown and sculpted for a bigger challenge than just declining fisheries. We face a global problem whose dark underbelly shadows all the coral reefs of the world, all of the industrialized fisheries, and all of the lakes, reservoirs, rivers, and estuaries on every land mass and nation on this planet. It is the problem of our planet supporting way too many people. All of them want to lead affluent lives like so many Americans, Europeans and a few others already do, as profligate consumers of food, energy, and "stuff." All of them want to exercise their newfound ability to change the world, but without first considering the unpleasant consequences likely to follow. And all of them can eventually get access to monstrously powerful technologies that enable them to do just that, at the press of a button. The death of the world's coral reefs, the depletion of the world's fisheries, the destruction of our freshwater systems in order to produce "clean" energy by damming all great rivers—these are just symptoms of a systemic disease: unbridled growth—growth in population, in affluence, and in power to transform and transmute. The path not taken would be one of growth in quality of life and equity, but at constant net levels of resource consumption.

Fishermen are bellwethers for the early symptoms of unlimited growth, telling us of depleted stocks, and of a changing climate as fishes head north or south to cooler waters where there might still be a hope of survival. They tell us of the mass extinction of creation that is right now unfolding before our eyes, as myriad species fail to find refuge from the human storm. People need such a bellwether because for all of our incredible talents, we share a huge and tragic flaw: denial. We see the need to change our behavior long before we do anything about it, and long after the time to react has passed. We damn the precautionary principle, put convenient belief before scientific truth, and cast our fate to the wind.

The wind is gathering. The fishermen are telling us so. And the ocean is bewilderingly complex. Fortunately, buried in that complexity is an astounding power of self-healing. Cod in New England may be having a hard go, but haddock responded well to our restraint. No-take marine reserves in many places are quickly seeing a rebuilding in the sizes and numbers of fishes, albeit these sanctuaries are way too small and too few. Urban harbors around the world that were once open sewers are getting clean again, as rivers and hills are reforested, and waste treatment centers built or modernized. And those who deny the reality of climate change are losing the argument amidst the din of killer storms and the wet of rising, acid seas.

We can bring back our ocean Eden. We need only back off . . . way, way back. We need only leave it the space it needs to heal.

PROLOGUE

A
SUNSET
REFLECTED

A second before jumping off the boat, Abu Sneida's body straightened. It seems that nobody, not even among the fellow Bedouins of his generation, remembers the seventy-year-old fisherman the way he was before his back became crooked and his gait waddling, as though the boat's undulations had somehow infected his feet and now followed him wherever he went. Abu Sneida dove into the reef's translucent waters and, as quickly as a shadow falls, laid his palms on the back of a huge sea turtle. He grabbed it, swirled with it for a little while, tangoing in tandem with the sunrays filtering through the waves, and, with powerful leg movements, forced it up to the surface.

For more than thirty years, Abu Sneida—the Bedouin fisherman—and I have sailed these waters in the Red Sea. Ras Muhammad ("the head of Muhammad") looks like the end of the world, located at the edge of a continental protrusion separating two gulfs, the Gulf of Suez to the west and the Gulf of Aqaba to the east. Here, the unique azure seawater sharply contrasts against the red sandstone cliffs and granite mountains of the Sinai Peninsula.

Hunting with bare hands in the transparent blue waters of the Red Sea.

The Old Man and the Sea Turtle Abu Sneida, my friend the fisherman.

Despite our long history, year after year, whenever I return to Ras Muhammad, Abu Sneida is respectfully introduced by Umbi, the captain of our diving boat, as "my friend, the fisherman." What being a fisherman means to Abu Sneida becomes clear at dinner every evening, when fish is served on the boat's kitchen table, and Abu Sneida modestly downplays our praises by saying, "Fish—that's the only thing I can do."

Together, we venture onto the deck to gaze at the sunset's reflection on the waters of the Red Sea. Nothing seems to change in this place, or so I like to believe. Abu Sneida disappears momentarily into the depths of our boat, and reemerges to serve us *fissikh*, a salted fish delicacy. He blows over a steaming cup of tea and talks of his extended fishing expeditions along the Red Sea coast. Here, in this time, in old Abu Sneida's voice, the ten-year-old boy who ventured on his first fishing trip lives on. Abu Sneida's father fell chronically ill after his boat capsized in a storm, forcing him to swim all night until he finally arrived at the shore exhausted. Despite being treated with all kinds of traditional brews of medicinal herbs and goat butter, he never regained his strength. It should have fallen to Abu Sneida's elder brother to take over for his father, but he had already drowned in these waters, his body never found. So young Abu Sneida was sent out to forge a living on the sea. He continues sailing in his world of stories until in his voice lives the veteran fishing boat captain he is now.

Abu Sneida's large sailboat drags a small fleet of smaller boats called feluccas, their fabric sails folded. Under these skies, in the light of the sunset, he sends out his feluccas to deploy their nets. Come morning, the feluccas will return with nets full of fish, some scared into their webbing by the commotion of the fleet. At the end of a successful fishing trip, they typically return to shore carrying 150 wooden barrels with some 450 pounds (over 200 kilograms) of fish stored between layers of salt. The salted fish become the same delicacy which we now, sitting on the deck, squish in our hands as we savor each delicious mouthful down to the salt that we lick off our fingers.

Abu Sneida turns to look at the turtle he has brought aboard. It is a male. Two crewmen are already carving it with huge kitchen knives, dissecting its organs. Abu Sneida smiles as they remove the genitals, and, as if reciting a recipe, says, "You let it out to dry, then grind it into a paste with a little honey and some herbs . . . a very powerful aphrodisiac. Then you sell it to a big sheikh up there in the mountains." He points to the red granite peaks in the distance and laughs. "He will pay a lot of money for this . . . and he'll want more."

The empty turtle shell emits a pungent odor, momentarily erasing Abu Sneida's semi-permanent broad smile. Then he shrugs his shoulders, saying, "To make that kind of money, you need to catch a lot of fish. Try to find that many fish in the sea today."

His few teeth are hidden behind sealed lips and his years suddenly show. He looks at the lights beginning to wink on along the beach as the sun gradually sinks behind the ridge, and nods. Perhaps, by using his powerful imagination, he is trying to strip the sea before us of all the cruise ships, yachts, and diving boats anchored to the beach; empty the extended coastline and riverbeds of the hundreds of new hotels with their myriad suites, nightclubs, malls, and entertainment centers brimming with the hundreds of thousands of people who frequent them each year. Perhaps the old fisherman is unaware of his exact age, and maybe the scenes of his life are laid out in a flat firmament of time, but at this moment, magic fails him. His aging eyes cannot ignore the sea changes in the world around him.

"Anyway," he mutters, "no matter how many fish you catch, you will get the same exact amount of money you used to get—only now it is worth a thousand times less." Once again, he smiles at me. "Come to think of it," he says, "what do you know about it? You've never caught a single fish in your life." Laughing, he adds, "But, really, you also catch fish, only yours never stink." Pulling on the strap of the camera hanging on my neck, he sighs. "And never grow old."

I've lived on the sea for over forty years. When asked about my profession, my late father used to say, "He takes pictures of fish," then would proudly add, "and sells them too." Like Abu Sneida, I, too, sometimes try to use my imagination to strip away the signs of change in the twilit reflection on these waters. But in my photographs, filtered through the portals of time and trapped in the web of memory, I see the story of my life, and the change to which I have been witness is impossible to imagine away.

When I look at the pictures, each photograph I have taken comes alive and reveals its tale. I collect these tales and bind them together: a compilation of the distant places I have reached and the strange creatures I have met above and below sea; a frightening anthology of my near-death experiences underwater; a recounting of the hasty decisions I have made in my career—my failures and my successes.

But beneath these collections of photos, which together chronicle my career, lies a story of change that is reflected in each and every picture I have taken as if this had been my original intent from the first moment I dove in with my camera. It is a story where, before my very eyes, causes and effects inhabit the same plain; a story in which our human actions live side by side with their impact on the oceans I have known and loved.

PART I

IN SEARCH OF BEAUTY AND AWE

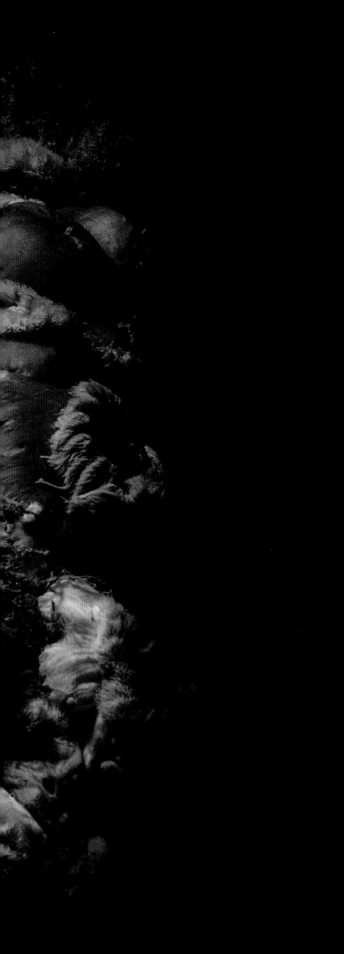

FIRST CONTACT

PRIMORDIAL SOUP: NEW ENGLAND

"It's really very simple," said my friend as he pointed to the diving regulator. It was a sunny day in Marblehead, Massachusetts, and we were about to dive into the cold waters of the Atlantic Ocean. "Put it in your mouth. Being a science teacher, you know all about respiration, don't you?" He laughed.

True—at the time, I was a science teacher at a Boston junior high school. I knew these waters from countless free-diving trips during previous summer holidays, but free dives simply involved holding your breath in the cold water to test your tolerance. So to me, the idea of using a regulator, of *breathing* underwater, was contrary to nature and all of my personal experiences so far. A minute before he dove, my friend said, "Remember, it's very simple. Suck it in, push it out, and when the air runs out, just go back up." Then he disappeared right under my nose. While I stood there hesitating, the air bubbles rising after him disappeared as well.

Sea raven, Rhode Island A "devil" in its throne of sea anemones, this sea raven actually sits in the middle of a torpedo firing tube of the U-853, a German submarine sunk off the coast of Rhode Island mere hours before WWII ended. (opposite)

A graceful pregnant Caribbean reef shark ready to give birth, Freeport, Bahamas. (pages 26 – 27)

Marblehead, Mass. Jeff Rotman at age 22, spearfishing in the Atlantic Ocean.

I remember that moment with perfect clarity, as I finally dove with millions of eyes watching me—the eyes of all the fish in the Atlantic.

As I plunged beneath the water, my hand instinctively reached for my diving knife. In those days, it was a machete-sized knife, suitable for any number of applications, but not quite suited for its actual purpose in this instance, which was cutting fishing lines and nets in the event of entanglement. At that moment, as I inhaled my first breath underwater, I saw nothing, not even my friend who had promised to watch out for me. I exhaled. My diving partner had told me that a diver's talent is measured by the amount of air he breathes, or, rather, that he does not breathe. The greener you are, the faster you breathe and the faster the air runs out.

I held my breath, not because of good training, or because I was awed by what I saw underwater, but because of the condensation that was gathering inside my diving mask. A brief moment passed before a heavy blow landed on my head, tearing the mask off my face. With salt-burnt eyes I faintly saw the blurry form of my buddy. With or without a mask, it is difficult to see much in the murky pea soup of New England's summer waters. Blindness, wrote Jorge Luis Borges, the Argentinean author who lost his eyesight at the end of his days, is not black obscurity, but rather a greenish, hazy cloud. I was diving blind.

It took a while before I realized that the fuzzy form of my friend was trying to show me something. I kept breathing wildly, anxiously, emptying my tank too quickly. What my friend demonstrated was simple—clean up the mask. I could have learned it in a basic diving course. But I had not taken a basic diving course—in those days, you weren't even required to get a diving license before diving! Somehow, though, I managed to clean the mask, and with a dwindling supply of air in my tank, we kept diving.

When we got to a depth of 33 feet (10 meters), I could no longer see the surface above. Looking down, all I saw was a dark and mysterious abyss. I was very uncomfortable. I began hyperventilating as I begrudgingly returned the "OK" sign, indicating that we could continue down. As we descended along the thermocline, through colder and colder waters, I became more frightened. My suit started compressing and I grew heavier and heavier from the water pressure. I was dropping like a stone toward the ocean floor.

The water was very cold at the bottom and visibility was terrible because previous divers had kicked up the silt resting on the ocean floor. I could hardly see a few feet ahead. All I could do was keep my eyes locked onto my friend's fins as he slowly swam around in front of me. I couldn't think. I was so cold that I was shaking like a leaf and I was consuming air at an alarming rate. The dive, my first dive, lasted about twenty minutes and all I saw was my friend's black dive fins and lots of dark brown silt.

But I kept diving. To recover my honor, at least in my own eyes, I showed up at the beach every morning like a good student. Each day during that summer holiday, I strapped

on my weights, hoisted my heavy tank, tied my knife to my calf, braved the beach breaks, crossed the pointy rocks, and got into the cold water. On even the hottest days, surface water temperature there doesn't top 68°F (about 20°C). And down near the bottom of the deep thermocline, it is never more than 40°F (4°C). Diving there was a true test of grit, "gorilla diving" as New Englanders call it.

But I had adopted the attitude of no pain, no gain. I played football in military college, and defensive tackles like me know better than anyone else that you just have to push through the limits your body tries to impose. When I started feeling the cold—and it didn't take long to feel cold there—I would try to shut down the torment by pressing an imaginary "stop" button, giving myself a second wind, a chance to steady my breath and continue. And, as in other sports, habit breeds addiction and you have to increase the dosage—longer, deeper, colder. I was told that if I could learn to dive in the cold, rough waters off the New England shore, I'd be able to dive anywhere. How prophetic those words would turn out to be.

Atlantic wolffish, Eastport, Maine
This fish is about to crack open a whelk with its powerful "canine" teeth. Particles in the photo reflect the poor visibility of the North Atlantic waters; you can hardly see the end of your arm if you hold it out in front of you.

BLUE WATER HUNTERS

The true athletes, the objects of my admiration, are not scuba divers like me, but free divers who enter the water with only goggles, a snorkel, and fins. Weighted perfectly, their hearts slowed to an almost unbelievably low rate, they are the best of the best when it comes to skin diving. When they dive, there isn't even a ripple on the surface. They are at one with the ocean.

I filmed some competitive free divers hunting in mid-ocean, about 300 miles (500 kilometers) offshore in pursuit of the biggest, most cunning predators of the sea. A few giant plankton-gobbling manta rays got used to their presence and took them for a ride: free-riding free divers.

During the dive, one of the hunters managed to spear a wahoo, a fish shaped like a barracuda. The spear went right through its gill plate and came out the other side. It immediately went into death shivers, giving off a very strong signal, audible to sharks—like a dinner bell. Sharks appeared out of the blue. Before the hunter could haul in the catch, which was supposed to be our dinner, the sharks had torn the wahoo to pieces; only the head remained. It made the water "so sharky," as the hunters put it, that we had to leave.

Clear and Present Game

When I started, there were only three kinds of diving that you could do in New England waters. The first option was to wreck dive, which means exploring sunken ships, of which there is no shortage in those treacherous waters. I have done my fair share of wreck diving. I even dove onto a German U-boat off of Rhode Island once. The U-boat had been sunk by depth bombs eight hours before the Second World War ended. All eighty-nine sailors aboard died.

Another New England diving option was spearfishing. For a while I did it, too. In those days, the sandy ocean bottom was covered with hundreds of flounder. Equipped with a pole spear, in no time at all a diver could bring back enough fish to feed a football team.

The third option was lobster (or "bug") diving. Eventually, I joined this third group. I wanted to catch the very thing that I could never afford to buy, to become part of the prestigious lobster-eating culture. It took just a few weeks for me to get quite good at finding lobsters—no mean feat considering they spend their daylight hours packed into small crevices, blending in with their surroundings in the dark green Atlantic waters. Soon, the menu item I always wanted but never chose became a daily staple.

It was a pleasure to usher my close friends into this "elite" lobster-eating culture along with me. All that was required for a fancy dinner was white wine (cooled nearly to its freezing point so as to disguise its taste and price) and a large pot. I took a huge pot from my late grandmother's kosher kitchen. Had she known that I used it to cook lobsters, which she considered profane (forbidden to Judaism) "creeps," she would have turned over in her grave. But use the pot I did—just thirteen minutes of cooking was all it took to achieve lobster nirvana. Often, my friends fell asleep at the table, replete of protein and alcohol. The few who stayed on for the morning meal of lobster omelets and lobster salad shared the belief that there was no more potent aphrodisiac than lobster. Perhaps its sway was an effect of some mysterious chemical compound flowing through its flesh, or perhaps it was simply the satisfaction of giving in to expensive taste.

I began to see my daily diving as a kind of "training ground." Each entry into the water was an opportunity to become a better diver—and hunter. The ocean and its lobsters were mine, claimed by my blood, toil, and tears. Young or old, large or small, male or female, I didn't mind; they all tasted the same to me. I would collect my booty, get out of the water, then lie back and melt in the hot sun to catch my breath and enjoy the feeling of success. So it was, one afternoon, when two middle-aged men skipped in my direction over the beach rocks and accosted me: "What do you have in that bag?" I was very proud of my catch, and so exclaimed, "Lobsters!" They asked if they could see them—as they flashed their badges: GAME WARDEN. My pride, so it seemed, was misplaced. They asked for my license. I didn't even know you were supposed to have one. To make things worse, thirteen out of the sixteen creatures I had bagged were under legal size.

I was led to the Gloucester Police Station. My $568 fine was an unimaginable amount of money—enough to have sponsored a field trip for my entire class to an upscale lobster joint.

When they let me go, I headed home. On the way, I stopped at a diving gear store. Browsing the shelves, I searched for something, anything, to help compensate for the loss, to distract me from my stolen ocean. And then I heard from the counter: "It's really very simple. Foolproof—all you have to do is push the button." "It" was a Nikonos underwater camera. I bought one.

Blackback flounder, Gloucester, Mass.
Early in its life, this flatfish swam upright, with one eye on each side of its head. Later in its life cycle, the fish lay down on its side; the lower eye, rather than stare forever into the featureless sand, migrated around the flounder's body to join the other eye.

Pause, Picture: A Silent Moment

The images were waiting for me. Like a hunter always focused on the target, I edited them all out of my consciousness while I was diving for lobsters, but I knew they were there: living creatures, unusual rocks, dark crevices, all just waiting to be captured. Or so I thought when I entered the water with my camera for the first time. All I needed to do was reawaken the previously rejected images from the depths of my memory and the fathoms of the ocean.

Gloucester, Mass. Matthew Rotman—Jeff's son, at age 11—holds a 13-pound lobster. (opposite)

American lobster, Gloucester, Mass. Strong claws and a hard protective shell make this lobster a formidable opponent. It has been called "the gangster of the sea," thanks to its aggressive look and territorial nature. (above)

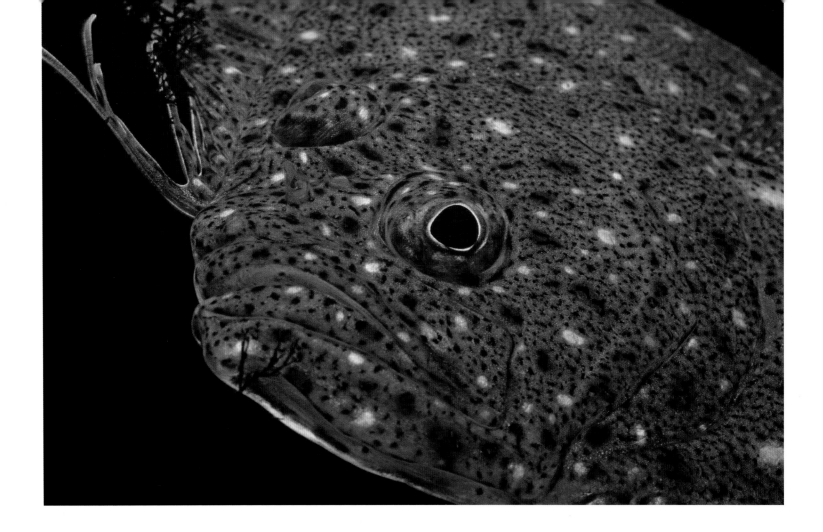

Windowpane flounder, Gloucester, Mass. Whether a flounder is right- or left-eyed is species-specific. After one eye migrates from the lower side of its body, both eyes are used to detect predators and prey.

However, it is one thing to look for something specific you know and want (to eat), and quite another to look for something unformed, an inchoate composition amid New England's pea-soup waters. I didn't know how to look. Was the key to cover more ground—did I need to move my fins faster to cover greater territory? Or was the key to be patient—to stop, observe, and wait? The longer I went without success, the more obscure and intangible it became. In those first moments, with the camera strapped around my neck, I asked myself the question that was to reverberate throughout my career: "What on Earth am I doing here?" Paradoxically, asking that question seems to keep me right where I am, not spur me to change course.

I don't remember what I photographed in that first dive, and even if I had the film to review (which I don't), the photos would likely reveal scant clues—light reflections, blurred lines, and shadows. I do remember the cold and my shaking hands, however. You can't train your body to withstand hypothermia, just as you can't train it to take shark bites and keep swimming. But with practice, I have mastered enough to maintain one stable fingertip, enough to exert a soft click on my camera. I also remember how hard I found it to stay still. Photography, unlike hunting, is about stillness, and it's not simple for a football player to marshal all his bursting energy and rein himself in. I wanted to make this a sporting challenge, but how many sports are there that test you for your ability to remain still?

Looking back, I don't recall when photography and diving stopped being challenges in themselves, and instead became secondary to my burgeoning interest in the objects and organisms of the seas that were revealed before my eyes—once I attained enough stillness and skill to find them. The thousands of pictures I have shot in these frigid waters over the years are laid out in my mind's eye with no temporal significance. But somewhere, above all of them hovers a kind of embryonic excitement harkening back to those first few experiences diving with my camera in the New England waters—live memories, vital and kicking.

Sea raven, Gloucester, Mass. In my opinion, this creature is one of the most gorgeously bizarre-looking fish on our planet. Its fleshy beard blends into the New England coastal environment, especially in the intertidal zone, amid beds of the red algae called Irish moss.

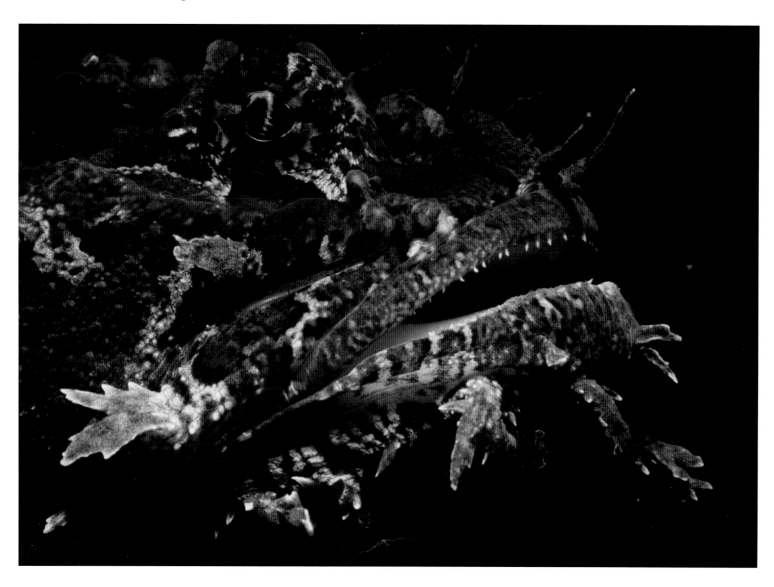

I do recall the unique moment when I was holding my breath, not to challenge myself or to save air, but to listen to the last bubbles rising from the regulator and dissolve above me. I heard nothing in the stillness that takes over after them, and realized that this silence around me was a world unto itself.

Perhaps, in search of that memory, I keep revisiting New England's shores, like a turtle that has hatched in their sands. And, perhaps to reawaken that charm, I take my children with me and watch them as they walk along the beach with a bucketful of water, just like I did in my own childhood. Seagulls scream in the background, and my nose catches that wonderful scent of the receding sea at low tide. Our pants rolled up, bare legs in the freezing water, we skip over the sharp rocks and hunt in the tide pools on the granitic boulders that border the beach. There, we fill our bucket with periwinkle snails, hermit and other crabs, sea urchins, starfish, and mussels. Occasionally, one of us finds a horseshoe crab washed up on the beach. After a storm, there is much more to choose from: many different and beautiful types of seaweeds, maybe a dead skate, or a dogfish shark, a cod, or a flounder that would be immediately fallen upon by seagulls. We return home, our bucket full, and keep our catch until the treasures smother the house with their intolerable stench.

When we swim, I take pictures of my children underwater. I shiver in my thick wetsuit, waiting for them on the bottom as they free dive in their bathing suits and swim toward me with powerful movements, seemingly oblivious to the cold. They know they're not allowed to ask me for air. Compressed in my tank, it can blow up their lungs if they don't release it on their way up, to the lower air pressure on the water surface. And anyway, they would not want to dwarf their challenge.

Northern red anemone, Deer Island, Canada Guarded by the tentacles that bring food to the anemone's mouth, these rosy puckered lips also offer the photographer an elusive prize.

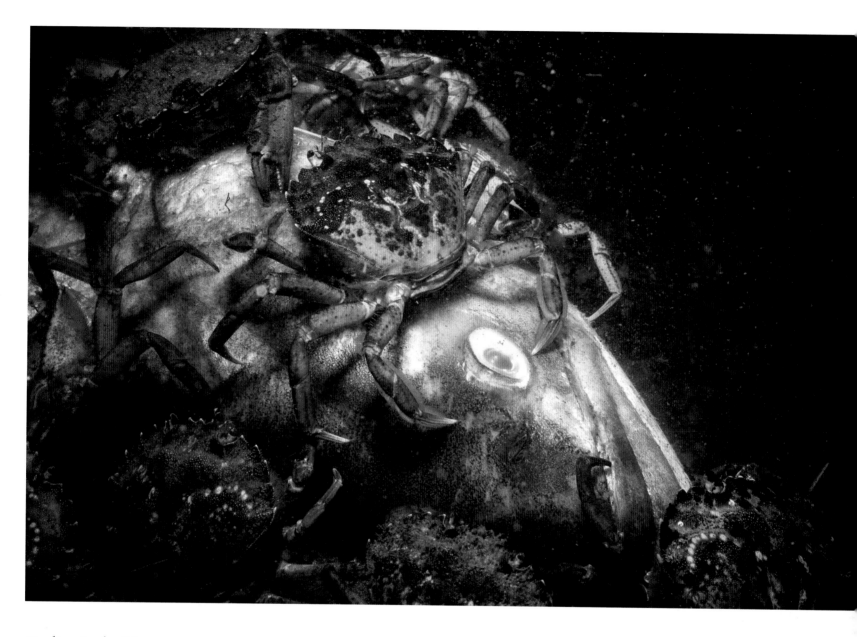

Reeling in the Line

I became infatuated with diving. Every summer when I'd return to the sea, my knowledge and understanding grew, and my photographs became sharper. What I discovered at the bottom of the ocean, I began researching in books; and what I saw in those books, I sought in the fathoms. Soon, diving just in the summer was not enough for me. So I would leave the school where I taught and drive an hour to the shore—even in winter.

In below-freezing temperatures, beyond snow-covered rocks, I would enter the water, the weights pulling me down into the warm embrace of 35°F (2°C). As nature would have

Green crabs scavenging a dead pollack, Gloucester, Mass. Sea scavengers rely on locating dead food by taste, smell, and even sound. The noise of a dead animal hitting the sea floor creates sound waves in the water that alert scavengers even hundreds of feet away.

it, the colder the air is, the clearer the water, because the plankton population dwindles. Also, as the air cools, fewer people visit the beach. The million eyes watching me were no longer there, and in that silent world, away from the breaking waves and howling wind, the frigid temperatures were just another obstacle to conquer.

I would concentrate on getting my shivering under control, and wait. I dove with only one camera, capable of taking just thirty-six photos per trip, so I needed take my time and find just the right subject for each photograph. If I pressed the shutter too quickly, too impatiently, the dive would end prematurely. Where once I was a temperamental tourist, skipping from destination to destination to pick up the sights, I became a patient observer, sitting on the bottom of the ocean, watching the comings and goings of the ocean-dwellers familiar to me from our previous encounters and from the books I devoured.

On a dive, there is a difference between stumbling upon something never before seen or known, and playing hide-and-seek with something familiar. Both forms of discovery make me very happy, bringing me warm satisfaction as if from a release of latent heat stored within the bodies of the creatures I capture. But the satisfaction differs. With the first type of discovery—the discovery of the previously unknown—the satisfaction is achieved only after doubtful hesitation. With the second type of discovery— or really, rediscovery—the joy is immediate. But it wasn't just sea life that I discovered: I also discovered myself, my joy.

In those slowly crystallizing waters, I became a happy man, and I shared my happiness with my students. I showed my pictures to the children at school; I even managed to take them on field trips to the beach. Some of those young Bostonians had never seen the ocean, and I got to introduce them to the magic: the sights, the scents, the open vistas. There, we'd take pictures together and my students came to know the magic of film. Waiting for pictures—those etched in memory and those that have become a living story—to materialize, is waiting for the "proof" of what you saw, like the testimony of a childhood stored in a time capsule. In those days, photographs

Matthew, *left*, Jeff, and Thomas, Rotman, Gloucester, Mass. circa 2012. (above)

Codfish, Gloucester, Mass. (opposite)

took about a week to get developed. During this time, the film's content often was forgotten or mutated into a different story. But like opening up a time capsule, looking at the photos brought us right back into the magic of the moment. This magic is still stored in the thousands of slides I occasionally dig out of their dusty boxes. The images are timeless, stored moments from years ago or just yesterday, waiting to come alive.

Many photographers, myself included, swear by the quality of film and its advantages over digital photography. It is a fact that ever since film has fallen out of use, a lot of money and knowledge has been invested in trying to recreate its quality in the new media. But I know that whether these efforts are deemed a success or not, the magic of film will never be recreated. All fisherman know this feeling. For them, it comes during the enchanted time that elapses between the moment they feel the tug on the line and the moment they pull the fish out of the water. Although the fishermen know the water and the fish they are targeting, they never know just what will actually arise from the deep— a prized and edible fish, a formless pile of algae, or just a rusty can. The anticipation is ritualistic.

For me, I reel in stories with a camera. In total silence, I hold my breath and don't let go until I hear the click. Following a dive, and always with some trepidation, I open up the camera case. After verifying that no water has seeped in and ruined my camera for good (as is all too often the case), I finally relax when I see the film, sealed tightly and securely. Over the years, I have gradually increased my load to up to ten cameras per dive (360 photos), and when my journeys took me far away from the only development lab I trusted, these rolled up stories would accumulate into a veritable trove. I carry the film, sealed within Ziploc bags, through train stations and airports, my anticipation strung out until finally, with intense and long-delayed joy, I can examine them on my studio light table back home.

The Fruits of the Moment

Somewhere within that same time frame, when the course of my life changed, hovers the moment when I chose to, as my father always liked to phrase it, "take pictures of fish" for a living. Even when I lay out my photos, early and recent, and try to reconstruct the moment when underwater photography became my *job,* it eludes me. I can see how I have vacillated between choice and doubt; this constant tension comes through even as the subjects of the photos change and the world changes around them. Perhaps it is this feeling that has kept me in this profession so long.

Perhaps there was no singular moment, but instead many moments in which I became a professional. One such moment occurred on a dive back in the familiar waters off the North Shore of Massachusetts. I got into the water and quickly dove to the bottom of the ocean. I turned on the flashlight and made my way through the murk, my light on

THE ONE AND ONLY GOOSEFISH

This is my one and only goosefish. Ever since we met on the bottom of the ocean thirty years ago, I've never seen another like it, except for a few unfortunate individuals trapped in fishing nets.

It was a freezing February night off the coast near Gloucester, Massachusetts. I dove in, and within the first few minutes, while trying to focus on the various items the ocean had on display, I saw the goosefish. At first, it appeared as a circle gently carved on the sand. What a splendid sight—a true rarity in these waters! Carefully, I swung around it and approached. The creature, trusting its camouflage, didn't budge, which gave me a rare opportunity. I shot it from several angles, using up the first six photos on my film roll. Such a treasure early in the dive, I thought, was a good omen, so I had better save the rest of the film for what was to come, since that's how records are made. I left it and moved on.

I soon realized my beginner's error.

Alas, I found nothing else worthwhile during that dive. On the way back, I tried to find the creature again, but to no avail. I felt as if I had slaughtered the proverbial goose after it had laid only one golden egg. I cherish these few photos for their beauty, rarity, and for the lesson I painfully learned—never stop shooting when you see something good. Never say you have already captured the best image you can get.

LIVING LEGENDS: GIANT OCTOPUS, GIANT SQUID

This is as close as real-life ocean creatures can come to the sea monsters of legend, the creatures that rise from below to embrace entire ships and drag them to the bottom.

In one of my deep dives in the Red Sea, I was ascending the length of the vertical reef wall when a mighty current drew me out into the open and forced me to grasp onto craggy crannies and slippery corals. I remember the intoxicating sensation that overcame me, a sense of total union with the visions, the quiet, and the movements of my own body. I don't recall the precise sequence of events, but I do recall that the following occurred, in some order.

I laid a soft hand on a protruding rock to direct my drifting body upwards, when suddenly the rock fluttered. A stonefish rose from under my hand, hovered for a second, and chose a different spot in which to settle just a few inches away. I was horrified. I looked at the fish, then back at my hand, searching for the stab wounds inflicted by the thirteen poison spines that rose from its dorsal fin right where my hand had just rested. A clock of borrowed time ticked wildly within me. Amazingly, my hand was smooth and apparently unscathed. As I calmed myself down, in the corner of my eye a stunning spectacle revealed itself. A giant squid appeared out of nowhere and, without a care in the world, swam gracefully, with harmonious and hypnotizing jet movements, into the deep.

Back on solid ground, nobody believed me. And in truth, I almost doubt it myself. A good friend said—insisted—that there were no giant squids in these waters and suggested that this vision might have been occasioned by some tiny dose of the stonefish's poison, just enough to make me hallucinate. And perhaps, he went on, I had been inspired by the psychoactive effects of the raptures of the deep. But I don't think so. Several years later, I shot film of a giant squid trapped in a fishnet, dragged from a depth of nearly 3,300 feet (1,000 meters) in the Red Sea.

The creature seen here is not a giant squid, but a giant octopus—a member of the same "sea monsters" family—shot in the Pacific. It was near Vancouver Island when my friend Jim Cosgrove (also known as "Mr. Octopus") pointed to a crevice in the reef wall whose opening was filled with a pile of empty scallop shells. When we directed our

flashlight beams inside, we saw shiny black slits reflecting the light. Jim squirted a chemical into the den, a respiratory irritant designed to annoy but not to harm the beast. Within seconds, a 65-pound (30-kilogram) octopus gingerly emerged. We found it repeatedly, and photographed it for an entire week.

A few years later, a friend told me he had photographed a Humboldt squid in the Gulf of Mexico. Unexpectedly, the creature wrapped its arms around him and pulled him toward the deep while tearing his mask and regulator off him. I don't know if my friend managed to escape through some feat of strength or whether the creature simply changed its mind at the last moment. Be that as it may, with hardly a breath left in his lungs he came up to the surface, climbed on deck, and without saying one word went into his room and didn't leave it for three days.

I wonder what stories will echo in my mind when I meet my next giant, and what shape it will take.

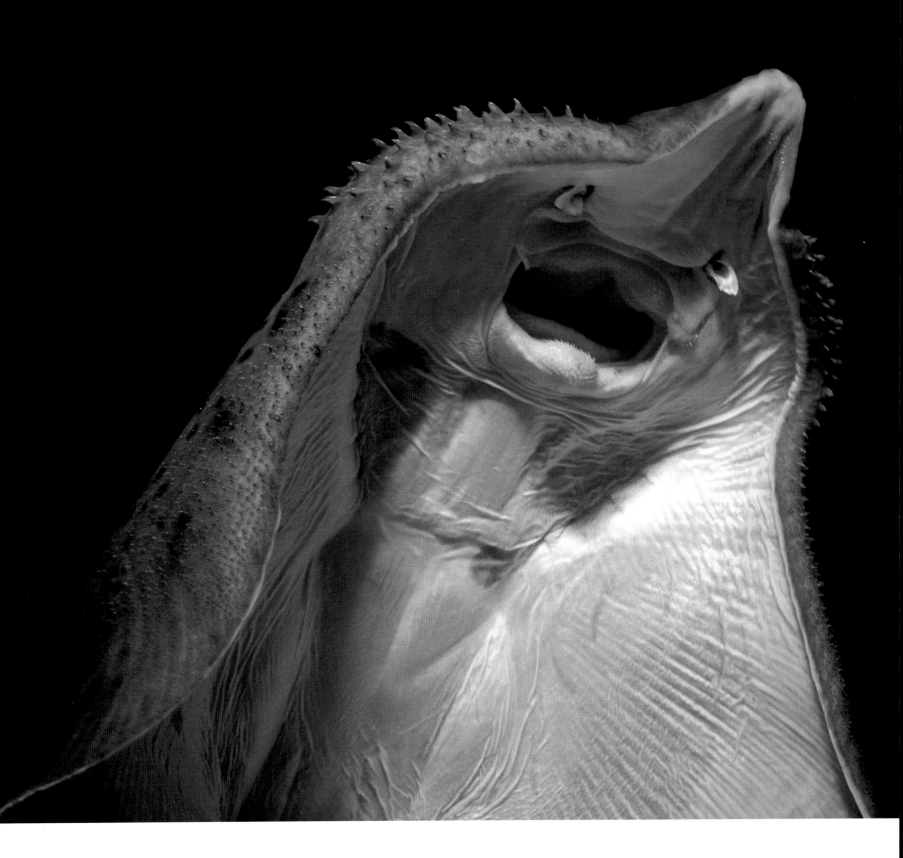

the lookout. The beam was momentarily smudged in the water. I let myself get lost. There is nothing more pleasurable than being lost within the boundaries of a familiar area, enjoying the adventure until my bearings are recaptured. On this particular day, my light suddenly split into what seemed like a whimsical lacelike pattern punctuated by shiny red dots. For a moment, I thought there was something wrong with my mask, but the patterns persisted even when I shook my head in disbelief. I had never seen anything like it in these waters: a swarm of tiny creatures hovering before me, slowly undulating in the water like a body with nothing to cover it but a transparent rainbow dress that swung around it gracefully.

My self-training took over as I disciplined my body, still shivering in cold and disbelief, into stillness as I readied a single stable fingertip to capture what I saw. The professional in me knew that the key would be freezing mid-hover and placing the camera at just the right distance. I swam after one of the mysterious organisms, following it out into the open water. It must have been propelled either by an underwater current or by the motion of my fins, because the more I chased, the farther from it I seemed to get. "One more shot," I told myself, "just one more."

In hindsight aided by years of subsequent experience, I can now identify the exact moment when I betrayed my training and ventured into the danger zone. There are a few strict guidelines that help keep a diver out of trouble: Never dive alone. Never stray off your diving plan. Never finish all the air down to the last breath. And never dive without a compass. No picture is worth dying for—after all, what good is a photo if no one will ever see and appreciate it? But on that day, there, in the water chasing after my mysterious quarry, I felt that no previous picture would ever equal the one that was about to be missed, the one that might be the unparalleled of all its predecessors—the one that nobody else had captured.

So I kept up my end of the pursuit. I clicked and clicked until the camera ran out of film. Only then did I let the creature glide away, and only then did I realize that I was truly lost and completely disoriented. I decided to swim up and look for the coastline, but the surface was blanketed with thick fog. I had no compass. All I knew for certain was that I was somewhere in the Atlantic, somewhere between the shores of New England and the rocks of Great Britain. The air outside was freezing.

I dove back down. I have found that the most stressful thing I can tell myself is "don't panic." Those words always seem to open the door to terror. So I breathed from the tank as calmly as I could and looked at the pressure gauge to see how much air I had left.

When it comes down to it, air is all a diver needs and I had enough left for any decision I could make, or so I felt. Panic was abandoned. St. Ives, here I come! I ascended with the regulator in my mouth so that I wouldn't have to fight the waves to breathe, but could instead just let them carry me to shore—any shore. After a while, I hit a rock. It was the

Little skate, Gloucester, Mass.
During the spring months I have seen the bottoms of coastal New England entirely covered by these remarkable creatures with their hallmark "wings" gracefully floating along the ocean floor.

sweetest pain to ever to visit my limbs. To climb the sharp rocks against the undertow, I let go of my weight belt, and then my tank, and finally my regulator. In the ecstasy of the moment, I toyed with the thought of going back to find my gear the next day. But I didn't really care. The camera was still around my neck, intact.

As usual, it took a week for the photographs to be developed. When I finally got them, there was nothing of note except for two "warm-up shots" of some kind of fish on the ocean bottom. Everything else was just unfocused blackness. Only later did I learn that in additional stillness, the right light direction is required for success.

Years later, I came across the creature once again. This time, I got my photo. By then, I knew what it was, a magical seafarer worthy of its name: the sea butterfly. The tiny one pictured here is a creature of the deep, food for giant baleen whales. It was pushed up and toward the shore by the blizzard of 1978, only to be captured by my film, frozen in time for all to see.

Sea butterfly, Gulf of Maine, Mass. Only one inch long, sea butterflies are food for giants—the baleen whales. Normally these tiny creatures are found in large numbers in pelagic waters well offshore, but this individual was probably blown in towards the shore by a blizzard. (above)

Atlantic rock crab, Gloucester, Mass. The larger male is holding onto a female that has released a pheromone to attract her suitor. The male will carry her around for weeks in order to mate after she has molted. (opposite)

ALADDIN'S CAVE: DISCOVERING THE TROPICS

The Lure of Beauty

Jacques Cousteau was in town! The guru of diving and undersea photography was in Boston. Jacques Cousteau, the man who had invented the Calypso camera (the ancestor of my Nikonos), had come to deliver a lecture at Harvard University. From the audience, I recognized some of the slides on the screen from books and magazines, but a certain connection had been missing up until now, a tangibility lacking. It was Cousteau himself—a deity among divers, with a foreign accent and simplicity of vision and technique—who made this connection for me.

After the lecture, I dared approach him. He was surrounded by people asking questions and vying for attention. When my turn came, there was only one question I wanted to ask: "Where's the best place to dive?" He smiled and thought for a moment before asking, "The most *beautiful*?" as though correcting me. "My happiest hours have been spent beneath the beautiful waters of the Red Sea."

Beauty. That word resonated within me as if it had been a chord already tuned, waiting for the proper moment to be struck.

I guess I had not been aware of it. As when peeping through a keyhole to see forbidden things, it can be difficult to turn away from the strange and scary. Over time, the object of your gaze transforms, and sometimes even the ugly turns beautiful. Even then, in the few photos I had managed to collect, beauty became a new prism and screened the images in a different spectrum.

Scalefin anthias, Sinai Peninsula, Egypt Scientists estimate that in some parts of the world, there can be as many species of fish per two acres of coral reef as there are species of birds in North America—that's more than two thousand.

BREATHTAKING: SAPPHIRINE GURNARD

At 130 feet (40 meters) in the Atlantic, near Brittany, France, I was photographing my first gurnard, or sea robin. It was cold and I was wearing a dry suit with no buoyancy compensator vest (also called a "BC"). The suit was the BC. I didn't come across the sea robin until the end of the dive. Even after I pulled the rod on my tank to activate my reserve air, which I do at the start of my ascents, I continued to shoot, wanting to get just one more photo . . . then just one more after that. . . .

I became so completely engrossed in photographing this wonderful gurnard that I forgot to ascend. All of a sudden it became hard to breathe; I was having trouble drawing air into my regulator. I sucked in but nothing came. I bolted for the surface. At about 65 feet (20 meters) I was able to suck in half a breath, but I knew that I was ascending much too fast and that it was important for me to release any air in my lungs so I wouldn't embolize, causing an air bubble to get into my brain. Of course, releasing air is easier said than done when you don't have any air to take in.

I came perilously close to passing out, but finally managed to reach the surface and inhale the sweetest breath of fresh air I think I have ever experienced. But I was able to enjoy only a few breaths before I realized that I was sinking. Without the BC, I was too heavy. I had to release my weight belt, but it was a French belt; I was unfamiliar with its buckle and could not get the damn thing to release. I was about to be pulled under—I was going to drown.

Lucky for me, the captain of my dive boat saw that I was in trouble. He cut his anchor line and got close enough to throw me a life ring. He saved my life. I couldn't have stayed on the surface for more than few seconds longer. That was a very strong lesson that I will never forget . . . till the next time I see my first sea robin.

I packed my rucksack, sleeping bag, and photography gear, and crossed the ocean to reach the Red Sea.

Pictures of tropical reefs were well known to me by that time, but I looked at them contemptuously. They were unbearably easy to shoot, unbearably beautiful in their composition. Where was the challenge? It was a sort of Bostonian boastfulness: "Look at those photographers in their bathing suits . . . All they need to do is put the camera down and let the photos flow in."

Now I was the one in the bathing suit, in the sunlight waiting for the photos to come. I opened my eyes beneath the water and felt like shouting: "I can see! I can see!" All thought escaped me and my preconceived self-perceptions dissolved. The beauty that surrounded me melted away everything I thought I knew about myself. I was no longer a Bostonian, science teacher, diver, or photographer. I was hovering in a different world.

I sat down on the sand between the rocks of the reef, a column of blue water above me. The visibility! Sunshine, water masquerading as blue sky in front of me—a submerged horizon! I reached out for my pressure gauge, an instinct saved for the *end* of a dive, but now I clung to it to avoid losing my sense of time in that space. How much time did I have left to take it all in? In the water above me, people were snorkeling in their swimsuits. For the first time, I missed having a close friend with whom I could share the experience. I was thinking about the students in my science class. How would I ever be able to explain this without invoking some divine entity?

Some free divers came down to the reef and extended exposed fingers toward the corals. Here, the warm water made unnecessary the three-fingered, thick diving gloves that killed my sensation and dexterity. Thus, the stunning colors of the reef could be enhanced by an additional sense: texture. Thorny. Coarse. Smooth. Velvety. I laid my hand on the branches of a flat coral, spread out like a breathtaking brush. The sharp, stinging pain in my fingers has helped me to remember its name even now: fire coral.

Nursing my fingers, I hovered over the reef and took in the landscape before me. But then, all at once, it disappeared and I was desperately fluttering my fins to get back. An almost perpendicular wall cut the reef. Colors became blurred on the way down and the abyss gained ominous real-life dimensions. A chasm had materialized below me and a current was pulling me out into the open ocean toward the "deep blue." I batted my fins for all they were worth, swept the water with my palms, and finally made it back. I clung to a protruding rock, fighting the current, as my hyperventilation quickly emptied my tank.

Bottlenose dolphin, Dolphin Reef, Eilat, Israel For more than 20 years, a family of dolphins has lived at this center, where dolphins are used for therapy and tourists can swim with them. Scientists also observe the dolphins to gain a better understanding of how they cooperate to defend the pod, hunt for food, and care for their young. Here, Dolphin Reef founding member Maya Zilber plays with her favorite dolphin. (1996 Science Photograph of the Year, as named by the National Press Photographers Association and the University of Missouri School of Journalism) (page 55)

Glassy sweepers, Red Sea, Eilat, Israel Milling around in flowing, shifting swarms, small fish find safety in numbers. Large schools fill a predator's field of vision, making it difficult for the predator to focus on a single target. (above)

Newborn hawksbill turtle, Sipadan Island, Borneo With its thin, soft shell, a newborn turtle needs to be lucky to avoid detection by the legions of predators that await it in the open ocean after it survives the perilous journey from sand to sea. (opposite)

I spent the next sixty days, right up until my morning flight on the last day of my summer vacation, diving in the Gulf of Eilat (also known as the Gulf of Aqaba) in the northernmost reaches of the Red Sea. At first, it was three times a day, sometimes for two hours at a stretch, until my body almost collapsed with exhaustion. Then I discovered the local nightlife—that is, the undersea creatures that come out at night. And so I added night dives to my routine. Apart from diving, I left my home away from home, a tent pitched close to the sea on the beach, only for necessities like food and tank refills. Otherwise, I stayed in the tent to wait out the periods of non-diving time forced upon me by the diving

Ras-Um-Sid, Sinai Peninsula, Egypt
The ocean is an alien world. No matter how many times you dive into it, the feeling of first contact always awaits. (opposite)

Rainbow wrasse, Sinai Peninsula, Egypt
This flamboyant fish was caught in surprise after having been roused from sleep in a cave. Note its relatively small eyes, which indicate that this type of fish is diurnal, or active in the daytime. (above)

Red Sea, Straights of Tiran, Egypt
Asher Gal and Jeff Rotman prepare for a 3AM night dive in the open ocean to photograph pelagic creatures.

tables—the time necessary to ensure that all the nitrogen bubbles in my blood had dissolved.

During those long, lazy breaks, my body was at rest but my mind wasn't. Today, my kind of psyche, so highly charged with curiosity and restlessness, might be labeled with a psychiatric term or diagnosis, but back then, I had to self-treat. And so a new addiction was born: a kind of greedy, voracious need to take photographs. Like Aladdin's magic lamp, my camera became a source of wish fulfillment, a means to satisfy my desires. All I had to do was dive into the water and go from cave to cave in search of photographic treasure.

My tent quickly began to fill up with rolls of film, each containing promise, happiness, and pride. But then, perhaps as punishment for my hubris and greed, it was all lost. While I was out on a nighttime dive, my tent was robbed. Everything was taken: my sleeping bag, backpack, wallet, passport, even the tent itself, and—my bag of films! If this was divine intervention designed to teach me some kind of lesson, to slow me down and ease my obsession, it failed. The very next day I was back in the water. Once an addict. . . .

Over time, I fed my addiction with new magic lamps and lenses, thus expanding my possibilities. But I still felt limited: How could I manage all this abundance in thirty-six photographs? Seventy-two? Or any other multiple, for that matter?

I hired assistants, not only to ease the weight of loneliness in godforsaken places around the world, but to help manage the cameras that could no longer be carried around my neck. In this way, I met Asher Gal. Asher is the consummate diver, the big brother I never had. Diving with Asher means never having to worry about irrevocably crossing boundaries into danger; as a former Israeli Navy Seal, he knows when and how to cross them, and when and how to pull back. It takes tremendous effort for Asher to both withstand my attacks of over-enthusiasm and impulsiveness underwater and to correct me against my will, but thankfully, he is up to the task and has done it again and again.

Asher is my guardian angel. He is as present in my photographs as he is underwater, as invisible as are all things taken for granted until they can no longer be. Occasionally, I lift my head above the camera and see him, cameras hanging around his neck, hugging himself, perhaps because of the cold and perhaps to prevent his mind from getting lost in thought. Only in the transatlantic calls we make between voyages do I feel the urge to hug him, just like that. And from afar, I imagine him dismissing my sentimentality with a mocking yet kind smile.

ON THE EDGE OF A SCALPEL: SURGEONFISH

I had waited years for this voyage—a trip to the Brothers Islands, a pair of islands in the middle of the Red Sea, off the coast of Egypt in East Africa. It was a virgin reef paradise. From Sharm al-Sheikh in Sinai Peninsula, I embarked on *The Hurriya* (Arabic for "freedom"), a wooden boat owned by my Bedouin friend Umbarak, who is today a Sinai diving tycoon. We had to cross to the middle of the Red Sea to reach the islands. I had never sailed that far before, across the ocean by boat. I was truly shaken, both by the waves and by my awe of the navigation skills of a true mariner. This was the pre-GPS era, when captains were guided by the stars, the directions of the wind and waves, and intuition grounded in generations of traditional experience.

When we arrived at the port of Hurghada on the African Coast, we took a taxi and made our bumpy way to the shore across from the Brothers Islands. A little supply boat took us to the islands at dusk. The lighthouse guards were happy to see us, and greeted us with tea. But before I could drain my cup, I became eager to dive into the water—it was sunset, the magical changeover time. I couldn't wait for daylight. Surely, a veteran diver like me could afford to violate one of the best-known diving safety rules? The rule: Reconnoiter your diving site at day, before venturing into it at night.

Indeed, the reef proved worthy of its praise. I sampled what the area had to offer by hovering inside canyons, across forests of coral, and into dark caves. In one cave I found what I had been desperately looking for: slumbering reef fish. I clicked the camera to capture a close-up image. The flash scared some fish away and out of the cave. One of them, I quickly realized, was a surgeonfish. It defensively swept its tail—which has a razor sharp knife on either side—back and forth. As it went past my leg, a fleetingly pleasant warmth spread under my wetsuit.

Then sharp pain tore across my thigh.

I pointed the flashlight toward my leg and saw a greenish cloud oozing out. Blood takes on this color underwater when lit by a flashlight at night. It also has a distinct smell, all too familiar to sharks.

I got out of the water. When I took off the suit, my blood—once more its familiar color—flowed uninterrupted. The tiny scalpel on the surgeonfish's tail had cut a long, deep gash in my flesh. I pulled the wet suit back up in order to hold the wound together and apply pressure. Thus, minutes after it had begun, the diving trip ended and another one started—straight to the mainland for a prolonged visit at the local hospital to treat the infected wound. I emerged with six stitches on my thigh.

When I told the story to a friend, he chuckled and said, "Mann tracht, Gott lacht"—Yiddish for "Men plan, God laughs."

Spice of the Deep

I missed the sixties' LSD train. I was too square and, if I recall correctly, drugs weren't part of the average football player's routine. Definitely not at the military college I attended, in any case. But as the years went by, I made up for these lost experiences and found the perfect cheap and plentiful substitute for hallucinogens—air, or rather one component of it: natural nitrogen, straight from the atmosphere and pressurized inside a scuba diving tank. The only thing you had to do to get high was dive deep enough and inhale.

This high has two names, one beautiful: raptures of the deep, and one scary: nitrogen narcosis. Back in the day, I used to think that nothing could equal sweet nitrogen intoxication combined with the beauty of the Sinai Peninsula's coral reefs. Several trips to this part of the Red Sea followed my first. So I was familiar with the area, its reef, landscapes, lifecycles, nomadic guests and permanent inhabitants, corals, and fascinating flora and fauna. But this time, I came to do something unfamiliar. I came to visit places that neither I, nor anyone else, had ever visited before. I came in search of photos never before captured on camera. I wanted to discover the unknown. The destinations might have been the same reefs as in all my previous diving tours, but this time, I would go deeper, to a depth of almost 300 feet (90 meters)—right at the edge of human endurance, where one becomes susceptible to oxygen poisoning and could, without any warning, pass out. . . . Goodnight.

Asher and I set the objective for this photography series: to document the symbiosis between corals and other forms of life in depths of more than 250 feet (80 meters). We knew that, at this perilous depth, angels of the deep await.

Experienced divers often engage in ultra-masculine competitions that serve to answer a simple question: "How deep can I dive?" When this happens, you can never be sure which will prevail: common sense or bravado. In response to this perennial rivalry, Asher, who is often witness to these impromptu competitions, jokes that divers commit suicide by jumping directly from the height of their egos to the depth of their IQs. But neither Asher nor I were teenagers with a yen for extreme sports. Rather, diving was (and still is) what we did for a living, our lifelong career, and how we presented ourselves to the world. We rationalized the madness of our endeavor by thinking of it as a scientific expedition. We entered into this challenge together, making the plunge into the abyss holding each other's hands like Thelma and Louise in their final scene.

At our dive site, there was no need to venture far from shore to reach great depths. An almost vertical, gorgeous reef wall falls directly into the Gulf of Aqaba. It is an immense, deep gash in the Earth's crust between the African and Arabian tectonic plates, which have been slowly drifting apart for eons. Following this steep cliff downwards, it is impossible to miss the milestones along the way: a sequence of different corals whose dazzling colors and shapes mark the depth foot by foot, meter by meter, like a depth gauge carved into rock. Perhaps the benevolent sea nymph Hurriya herself awaited us below. Might she

School of barracuda, Kimbe Bay, Papua New Guinea Barracuda circling the diver to check what form of strange creature he is; this is a defensive behavior to confuse predators.

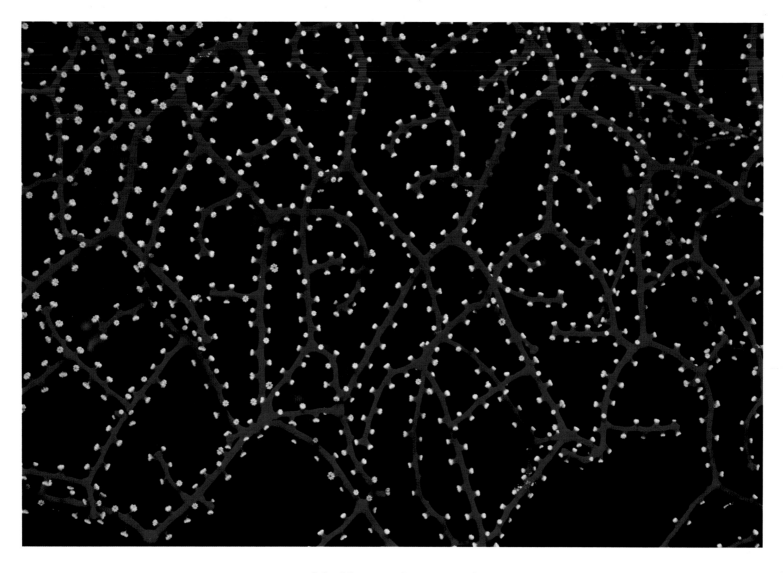

Scarlet sea fan, Palau Island, Micronesia Under my strobe light, this creature appeared to my eyes a stunning red, but the color red is the first to fade out as you go deeper underwater. The farther light has to travel through water, the more wavelengths are absorbed, and red has the longest wavelength of the visible spectrum. (above)

Tomato clownfish, Lembeh Strait, Sulawesi, Indonesia This clownfish lives symbiotically in an anemone. (opposite)

emerge out of the blue to welcome us to her maritime netherworld by kissing our life away as the high-pressure air crammed into our lungs turns into lethal poison?

We carefully laid out our plan, which would take place in stages over an entire month. The first dive went to 164 feet (50 meters), where rapturous intoxication starts. Here, consciousness is altered, or perhaps it is the world that is altered . . . or maybe it's both. At this depth, our sense of time began expanding as we paused to take in the beauty, while our joints absorbed the nitrogen building up in our blood. In the crystal-clear waters of the Red Sea, sunlight penetrates deeply. Visibility was good enough for us to see the unusual palette caused by filtered sunlight applying its velvet touch to all of the living creatures and inanimate objects within its reach. Like magic, a flashlight turns off the effect of the fading, shimmering light, and repaints everything in its original color.

Each day, our dives went deeper. We assumed that we were gradually acclimatizing our bodies to narcosis, getting used to it so that we would have enough sense left to break free of the dreamlike state it causes. We felt that we could maintain enough self-control and sense to avoid inhaling the water around us and losing sight of why we were diving in the first place.

On the last day of our trip, we started our final and deepest descent. We knew that time was the critical key. At that depth, we had to receive air at higher pressure and the tank would empty quickly. For us to have enough time to work, we removed the safety valves on our diving tanks and compressed a double dose of air into them during fill-up, resulting in two time bombs ticking outside and inside our bodies. Even then, we knew that our tanks would be completely spent after just a few minutes of exploration. So to make sure we had enough air to return safely—enough for more than two hours of decompression on the way back— we left two full tanks 50 feet (15 meters) from the surface. Here, at our first decompression stop along our ascent, we would exchange the empty tanks with the full ones, giving us enough air for the rest of the way. On our way down, we hung these safety tanks on a familiar reef slope so there would be no difficulty finding them. Then, as planned, we dove down to 285 feet (87 meters), only 10 feet (3 meters) away from that rapturous edge.

And there we were. The stillness was overwhelming— even our deep, frugal breaths did not disturb it. Then again, maybe we weren't breathing at all, but holding it so as not to mar the euphoria of the surroundings. Splendor like this, the tranquility of it, cannot be described in words.

We had only fifteen precious minutes before we had to start our return trip.

Bearded scorpion fish, Sinai peninsula, Egypt Master of camouflage and surprise, this poisonous fish is one of the most deadly fish in the reef. It sits quietly on the ocean floor like part of the coral. The venom in its spines is toxic to the nervous system and blood vessels of its victims, who never know what got them.

Despite the extraordinary feelings of amazement that overwhelmed me, I managed to shoot photographs. After all these years, it had become an act as natural to me as blinking. It helped that it was Asher who was in charge of the worrying. Like an eight-eyed sea monster, he had one eye on the air pressure gauge in his own tank, another on my gauge, a third on the diving computer, a fourth (on the back of his head) for sharks, an extra pair for spotting any detail I had missed that was worth shooting, a seventh to keep fixated on our journey back up to the surface, and an eighth—his mind's eye— focused on the hidden realm of his extraordinary instincts. These same instincts once caused him to launch himself from the deck of a diving boat directly on top of an oceanic whitetip shark that was about to attack an unsuspecting diver, saving her life. "Superman," I called him, and he humbly corrected me: "Superman, size medium."

Suddenly, Asher tore me away from a camera shot. He escaped his own brain fog and pulled me free of the deep roots that had grown out of me and into the reef. Our fifteen minutes were up. It would take another two weeks before I would see the developed photos. (I still lived in the Jurassic Era, you see, protecting the dinosaur we call film from extinction.) When I look at them now, knowing what happened, the stunning splendor of these pictures is enriched by the reminder of lives saved— my own and Asher's—thanks to Superman. ◆

Slowly we ascended, fighting the weight of the entire ocean above us. As the rapture of the deep

Tiny blenny, Red Sea, Egypt This half-inch creature lives on blue volcano sponge, at a depth of 280 feet. (top)

Squaretail grouper, Sinai Peninsula, Egypt A fearsome predator, the squaretail grouper acts during the twilight hours of dawn and dusk. Its slightly protruding lower jaw and small sharp teeth enable it to grasp prey firmly before swallowing them whole. (bottom)

started ebbing away, something else seeped through in its stead—apprehension. The world became clearer, and my fear intensified. It was time to pay for forbidden pleasures. Still, as I looked at the vertical reef wall on the long way back, I reminded myself that I was among the luckiest men on Earth. The profession I had chosen rewards me with riches extracted from the deep each time I dive. I tried to remain focused on the detail, as shade by velvet shade, the changing colors shifted in the penetrating sunlight. I zoomed in on the red, the green, the orange, the white, the black, and everything in between.

And then I saw Asher waiting for me, giving me the thumbs up. At that moment, I thought everything was OK. Fear faded and gave way to joy. We were approaching 50 feet (15 meters), a "business-as-usual" depth. We were just two hours and ten minutes from the surface. All we had to do was follow the protocol: fifteen minutes of decompression here; twenty minutes at 40 feet (12 meters), where we would see amateur snorkelers taking quick souvenir shots; twenty-five minutes at 30 feet (9 meters); thirty minutes at 20 feet (6 meters); and another long forty minutes at 10 feet (3 meters), where we would be able to see the bottom of the boat and fantasize about the post-expedition coffee awaiting us.

We kept climbing. From below, we identified our milestone on the cliff. Then Asher stopped in mid-swim, turned, and looked at me doubtfully. He usually does this only when he wants to reproach me for some stupid mistake I have made. But oh, God! Not this time. This time it was provoked by something far worse.

The reef was there. The milestone was there. But the tanks were not.

For a moment, we doubted our memory. Perhaps something had changed—the milestone in our head, or in the world, or both.

The euphoria of the deep was gone. At this depth, things are crystal clear, and I saw with perfect clarity that Asher was scared. I pictured nitrogen starting to gurgle in my blood. I saw the bubbles getting stuck in tiny blood vessels throughout my body, inflating and disconnecting main wires, disrupting nerve circuits. It's called "the bends," or brain embolism, and it's what I was going to suffer. Best-case scenario, I was headed for paralysis. I recalled a good friend of mine, a diver, who had succumbed to the bends and is today bound to a wheelchair, urinating into a bag hanging on his side. Unfortunately for him, he didn't have Asher by his side. And maybe, at that moment, Asher remembered that there was nobody there to back *him* up. He gave me the "calm down"—or "stay put"— signal, and I watched him ascend quickly to the boat above us.

Later he told me what he knew. He had three minutes at the surface, not a second more, before the dissolved nitrogen in his blood would turn into a gas. Three minutes to do what needed to be done and return to the safe depth of 50 feet (15 meters) below, where I was waiting.

Asher reached the surface, climbed the rear ladder to the deck, and took clumsy, ridiculous steps in his huge fins toward the diving tanks. He untied them, grabbed one,

Needlefish, Sinai Peninsula, Egypt
This school of juvenile needlefish appeared during the transitional period from day to night.

attached a regulator and tested the pressure, took another tank, looked for another regulator, found it, attached it to the tank, made the necessary tests, and then grabbed both tanks by their heads. With adrenaline pulsing through him, this "Superman, size medium" overcame their weight and his own fatigue and jumped back into the blue before somebody could ask him whether or not he wanted his coffee with sugar. Fighting against the air that filled his lungs and tried to push him upwards, he made his way down with a tank in each arm, until he got back to me.

With full tanks attached and air once again flowing, we now had two hours and ten minutes to tame the demons, to choke them in their nitrogen bubbles. One hundred and thirty minutes to reflect and restore calm; to wonder what happened to the tanks we had left behind and what had possessed us to make such risky and stupid decisions. This was the necessary time for our rehabilitation.

Today a storyteller lives to tell the tale, up from almost three hundred feet deep. Photographs also survive to remind us of the beautiful and of the forbidden.

That same day, an amateur diver, an honest man with a deep sense of purpose, returned the missing tanks that he had found "just hanging" in the middle of the water, two tanks probably "forgotten by two clowns," he said.

Changeover

A friend came to stay with me in my Jerusalem apartment. In those days, I was photographing a story about the bomb squad dealing with terrorist threats in the city—one of many photojournalism gigs I accepted in order to fund my expensive oceanic voyages. This was in the late 1980s, at the time of the First Intifada, the first Palestinian uprising against Israeli occupation, so tensions were high. Nevertheless, since this was my friend's initial visit there, he insisted on walking the alleys of the Old City. Wandering around the Muslim Quarter, we found ourselves in the Butchers' Market. There were very few shoppers about, so we took the opportunity to enter one of the shops to buy meat. A few seconds later, the owner looked outside and his entire expression suddenly changed. He urgently pleaded for us to leave.

Scarlet anthias, Red Sea, Egypt Picture yourself flipping a page in the book. In the flick of a fin, over an imaginary next page, all these fish drifting before you over the reef corals disappear. Then, turn the page quickly to one that is blank, dark. This is the power of that dramatic twilight clock.

TO THE END OF THE WORLD: BIKINI ATOLL

In 1994, *The New York Times Magazine* decided to do a cover story in commemoration of the fiftieth anniversary of the atomic bomb explosion on Hiroshima. Even in the pre-cellular telephone era, a determined editor could track you anywhere in the world. I was diving in the Red Sea when a messenger arrived at my boat, telling me someone was looking for me urgently. We went back to the beach, where a fax was waiting for me, asking me to call the *New York Times* newspaper offices ASAP. When we spoke, the editor told me about the cover story and that they wanted me to go out to the Bikini Atoll in the Pacific Ocean, where the United States had tested nuclear weapons in 1946, to dive onto the sunken aircraft carrier used in the test. "Somebody will wait for you there with all the equipment you need," she said.

In just three days, I did what Phileas Fogg and Jean Passepartout completed in forty: I traveled half-way "around the world." From Sharm al-Sheikh I flew to Cairo and from there to London where I boarded a plane to Boston—I had to stop at home for more gear. From Boston, I flew to Miami and from there to Guam, and then I hopped from one Pacific island to the next in a series of six or seven flights in light planes. Finally, a five-hour boat ride ended my journey.

When I reached the atoll, exhausted, I was happy to discover that someone had, indeed prepared everything I needed for the job down to the last detail: boat, fuel, food, a compressor, and complete diving gear. Obviously, a true professional was involved. And then, from a reclining chair on the beach, a figure stood up and stepped out of the shade cast by a parasol. I recognized him, it was Bill Curtsinger—a colleague of mine, one of my sources of inspiration.

He approached and, upon recognizing me, said in his understated way, "Oh, it's you. They stopped me in a middle of a shoot and asked me to prepare equipment for some kind of VIP who's supposed to arrive."

The street had become completely empty. Outside the shops, skinned sheep and cow carcasses hung on hooks next to other huge meat cuts. Their ominous red color was strangely in keeping with the air suddenly compressing around us. We stood exposed at the center of the narrow alley, not a soul in sight. Without any perceptible reason, everything had come to a total standstill.

We rushed out of the alley and left the Old City. It was curfew time. When we recaptured our breath, my friend said, "Changeover."

I knew what he meant, this deathly quiet.

A few days earlier, I had hosted him in my second home, the Red Sea. This time, I was diving off the reef at Sharm al-Sheikh, at the southernmost tip of the Sinai Peninsula. It was the high season, and throngs of tourists flooded the popular beaches and diving clubs in the Straits of Tiran between Sinai and Saudi Arabia. One late afternoon, I promised to take him to an isolated spot where he wouldn't see a single diver near him. I pointed to Jackson Reef, smack in the middle of the straits. Dozens of diving boats were anchored there, all tied next to one another in a long row. "You mean there?" He looked at me in disbelief. "It's a question of timing," I replied.

The sun had made its way to the craggy skyline of the Sinai peaks. "Within minutes," I said, "everyone will leave and the reef will be ours." My New Yorker buddy laughed. "If you find parking on Wall Street at 3AM, that doesn't make it an opportunity. Surely there's a reason why this place is empty at night." He pointed at several boats that had begun heading back to shore. Indeed, by the time we moored at the reef, the last boat had already sailed. We quickly jumped into the water—I didn't want to miss *the moment*.

Human eyes can hardly detect that moment when light begins to fade underwater. But we know the indicators in the environment—things start to change. I learned about this from my private teacher, Joseph Levine, a marine biologist by profession, but above all a friend (also, like me, a native Bostonian and avid Patriots fan). We used to live two blocks away from one another, but had to cross an entire ocean to meet. His experience benefited me now as I took my guest on a twilight trip on the reef, and marshaled my senses, honed as they were by Joe's observational skills.

When the reef clock strikes dusk, it is difficult to detect any noticeable change in the light, but if you lend the sea your ear, you won't miss it. The parrotfish stop gnawing on the algae-covered corals. Then, as one, they all

Blackfin barracuda, Kimbe Bay, Papua New Guinea With its fang-filled underbite, a barracuda may look scary, but its reputation as a dangerous creature is undeserved. After two days of my presence around this school, the barracuda stopped seeing me as a threat and allowed me to come within.

stand on their tails and perform a strange dance, almost
as if in celebration of a successful day's work, before they
line up in one long school and disappear into the deep.

The surgeonfish respond to the same inaudible cue,
as if the factory siren has blown and the working day
is done. They swim to the edge of the reef toward the
open sea, forming a tiny train that joins up with other
tiny trains en route. Then, in a splendid parade, they all
head toward Reef Grand Central Station. Over the next
few minutes the fish merge, perform an enigmatic group
dance, and leave behind a white cloud of egg and sperm
cells slowly drifting in the water. In a blink of a diver's
eye, they're gone.

At five minutes past dusk, other daytime fish stop
hunting. Some of them suddenly doff their resplendent
colors, don their pajamas, and go look for a place to spend
the night. The triggerfish, for one, anchors into a narrow
crevice, and uses the tiny thorn on his back for which he
is named, to lock himself into a rocky cranny so that no
nocturnal predator will be able to disturb his dreams (and
life) and snatch him out of the reef.

By ten minutes past dusk, it is impossible not to notice
the transformation. In one fell swoop, the reef is occupied
by a mysterious force, and the tension threatens to further
compress the air inside our tanks. Even if you hear the
noises of the bubbles you breathe out, it is impossible to
describe this sudden exodus other than as an eerie silence.
The alleys of the deep become empty, and remain so for
long moments, until one hour after sundown, the reef is
wrapped in thick blackness.

**Mimic octopus, Lembeh Strait,
Celebes Sea, Sulawesi, Indonesia**
A mimic octopus silently drops
down on unsuspecting prey.

IN PURSUIT OF A NIGHTMARE: STARGAZER

Whether to stand atop a mountain peak, catch a glimpse of a famous postcard-worthy monument, or fulfill a noble mission, people travel great distances, across continents and oceans, to pursue their dreams. But I crossed continents and oceans in pursuit of a monster straight out of my nightmares: the stargazer. The image of this monster was branded in my brain, distinguished from thousands of pages of images I had leafed through over the years. It hunts in a particularly ruthless way: Camouflaged in greyish sand, it leaps and unlocks its abysmal mouth, engulfing whoever has the misfortune of swimming above it. In my nightmare, the unfortunate soul is me. Perhaps mercifully, I die of fright just before it swallows me.

To confront my nightmare, I traveled to Lembeh, Indonesia, for night diving.

When first I poked my diving mask beneath the waters of Lembeh Strait, I knew I was in trouble. I thought that either my mask had somehow gotten scratched by sandpaper, or I was suffering from sudden-onset blindness. In reality, volcanic sand and grey silt rose from the strait's bottom, turning the water into a murky soup. I was supposed to spend a month diving here, but I couldn't see a thing. Luckily, my assistant for the trip, Roland, was accustomed to these conditions—and to diving with those who are not. Roland called himself a "spotter" and soon I realized why. On our first dive, he pulled me after him, stopped and pointed down to a place in the sand below us where a tiny branch of Gorgonia coral was growing out of the sand. On the coral polyps were two perfectly camouflaged pygmy seahorses the size of a pencil eraser. It was miraculous.

I didn't understand how he was able to do it, but time and again, Roland's index finger pointed the way through cloudy waters to creatures I had never seen, nor would ever have seen had it not been for Roland's keen eyes. I think he must have thought me hopeless. As I'd struggle to see what he saw so easily, he would just shrug his shoulders in bafflement and smile. But even though countless wondrous creatures had posed before my camera, I remained focused on the one that hadn't: the stargazer. Roland saw many stargazers, but I was adamant that I had to be the one to spot it. "I think of it as a challenge," I would tell Roland upon turning down his offers of help, but really, my stubbornness was borne from my need to recreate the mystical events from my nightmare.

Nearly a month of night diving had gone by and time was running out. "Look for two points shimmering in the light of your flashlight," Roland would advise me each time we got out of the water. "Two eyes are the only thing this creature exposes above the sand." And then, one night, in a mystical manner straight out of my nightmares, the stargazer revealed itself.

I was following a banded sea snake, a potentially very dangerous animal with venom similar to that of a cobra. I had spotted the snake when it surfaced for a breath of air. After spending a few minutes at the surface, it dove back for the bottom. Seemingly oblivious to my presence, the snake headed straight toward me, flicking a delicate gray tongue out of a lemon-yellow head. Swimming back and down with it, I was able to capture its image in the inky blackness.

Seconds later, when the snake touched the sand, I saw in the flashlight beam those two gleaming points that had eluded me for so long. I lit Roland's face and could see his eyes shining at me through his mask. He had spotted the fish, too. Roland moved an open palm, gesturing to fan away the sand and reveal my prize.

Over the next hour or so, I took more than a hundred photos of that fabulous fish that I would come to think of as my own private stargazer. I could have easily shot another hundred, but I ran out of film. Finding it difficult to say goodbye, I held it in the beam of my flashlight. And then, a moment before I broke away, it happened. Just like in my nightmare, the stargazer leaped out of the sand, opened a gigantic mouth and caught . . . something, before it disappeared. I didn't have a chance to see what it was, probably another fish attracted by my flashlight. I was just relieved that it wasn't me. My feeling of relief, however, soon turned to one of severe disappointment: I did not catch this amazing moment on film.

Had I been able to capture it, I could have had the photo of the century. As the stargazer disappeared with its prey, it left me with an impression on the edge of my memory, like a blurry smudge on a long-exposure film.

What Is the Shape of Darkness?

Every time I go into the water alone at night, the story of Bill Curtsinger comes with me. Bill is one of the world's top underwater wildlife photographers. On one of his dives, about 130 feet (40 meters) down in open water, he shined his flashlight on a tiny, almost microscopic creature of interest. As he looked for a good angle and prepared his shot, he was suddenly jostled as something rubbed against his back. He froze. He was able to assess the creature's size by the duration of the contact. It was big. As he recaptured his breath, he didn't need to turn around, light shining, to know what it was—nor did he dare. But he saw it nonetheless: a 16-foot (5-meter) tiger shark swimming away, leaving Bill to dive another day.

Painted anemone, Queen Charlotte Strait, British Columbia, Canada Close-up of this creature's mouth. (above)

Cup coral eating juvenile octopus, Sinai Peninsula, Egypt In the dead of night I came across this rare sight. A healthy octopus would never allow itself to be caught by a cup coral; this one possibly stumbled onto the coral. The nematocysts on the tentacles of the cup coral have paralyzed the tiny creature. (opposite)

Pacific cownose rays, Galapagos Islands, Ecuador This school in flight formation was my reward for entering the sea at sunrise.

Imagine entering the water at night after hearing Bill's story, and assume that, as in any oral tradition, the shark just kept getting bigger and bigger as it swims along the proverbial grapevine. Imagine a million submarine eyes gazing at your flashlight, attracted to it like moths. Imagine countless creatures drawn to the vibration and noise of the bubbles you make in that silent netherworld. Imagine losing contact with the reef and drifting down into a bottomless pit, with nothing to hold onto but hope.

The first time I dove at night, I was alone. All of my subsequent night dives have been reflections of that dive, one long film made up of thousands of flashes and one feeling.

Diving at night offers the photographer many opportunities that are not available in daytime. But all of these incentives are dwarfed by the one true reason why I do it: Because! Just because.

So now push away the visions of giant sharks, and try to imagine a world of colors brought to life and sustained exclusively by the ray of light you hold in your hand. Imagine a moonlit night with a white curtain caressing the water above you and a world of shadows shimmering around you, the wavelets playing with whatever little lunar light there is available. Imagine walking at night into a neighborhood known to you at daytime—the same streets, the same crossroads, the same houses—but all the neighbors are gone and new tenants are there to play in front of you and for you.

Diving at night "just because" has many professional advantages, I've discovered. At night, your ray of light is itself a focusing mechanism, isolating everything around it and enabling you to concentrate on the object in front of you. When taking photographs, this isolation lends a sense of confidence, a kind of illusion that you yourself are invisible. In fact, it feels as if the only things visible in the world are those that you light up, and even then, the whole scene can be turned off at the click of a button should you so desire. In that dark world, all the daytime creatures huddle inside the crevices of the reef. Some of them sleep so deeply that you can approach them like a thief and grab whatever you want; the treasures I take are their images, captured on film, fixing them in time in a way that grants them a sort of immortality beyond their natural years.

Of those creatures who do venture out at night, many are small or slow, relying on the protection of darkness and never straying out too far. Thus you, also, can stay put in the tiny bubble you have created for yourself. And the less you move, the better you can observe.

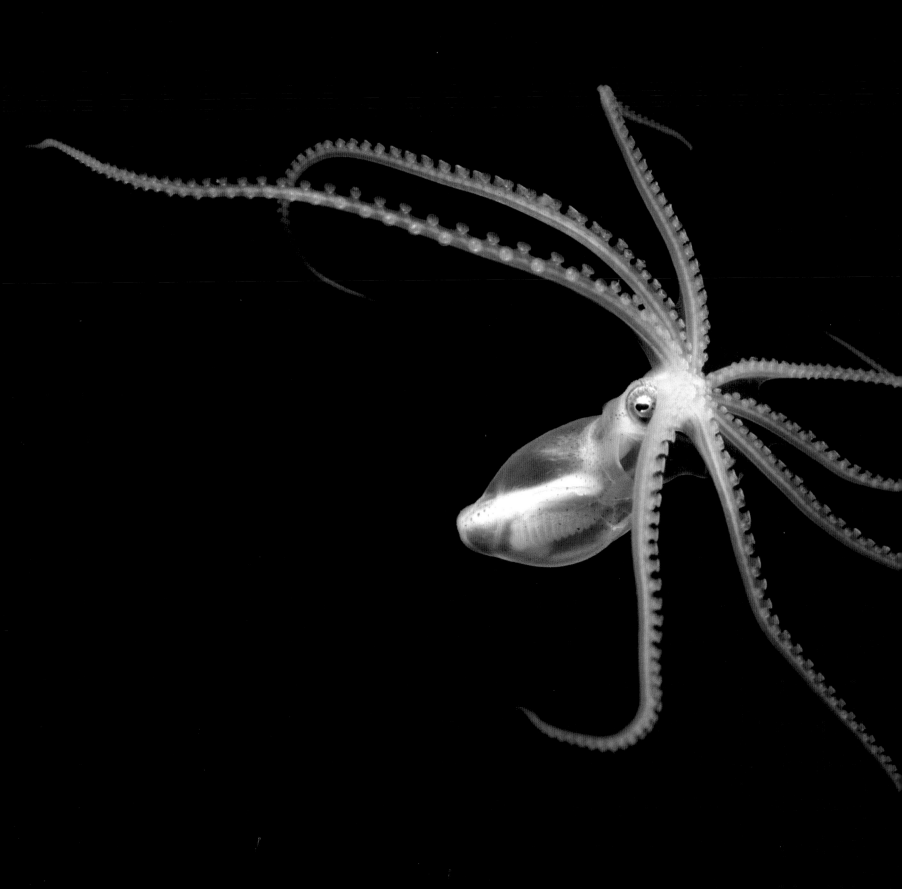

ARTIFICIAL MOON:
PELAGIC CREATURES IN THE RED SEA

Fishermen use constant lighting to illuminate the surface of the water and seduce fish to rise toward an artificial moon. My photographer friend Bill Curtsinger started using the technique for submarine photography; I borrowed it from him and wanted to try it in the waters of the Red Sea.

My diving buddy then, Ernst Meier, a photographer in his own right, built a cage and equipped it with two powerful lamps of two thousand watts each. We dove, protected by the cage, but before us lay a spectacle well worth dying for—or at least worth taking a risk. We left the cage.

Maybe by adding all the "just becauses" of all my night dives put together and taking the sum to the power of ten, I can hope to explain why Ernst, Asher, and I danced with joy when we resurfaced. It felt as if all the air compressed in our tanks was released in a single univocal, "Wow!"

In addition to the pelagic drifters swarming the waters and shining before us, our artificial moon attracted nocturnal migrators that travel half a mile or more (as much as a kilometer) vertically toward the surface at night. Everywhere we looked, animals were devouring other animals in a Lilliputian feeding frenzy. No sooner would our eyes lock onto a subject than it would disappear in a gulp. Asher noticed an enormous school of fish that had surrounded our cage. A moment later, it broke apart and then regrouped in a typical evasive action to escape a predator.

A smaller school of about twenty jacks circled below. Every few minutes they broke formation and rushed into the school with snapping jaws.

I stopped taking photographs and watched the extraordinary scene.

Pelagic octopus, Sinai Peninsula, Egypt

AN OASIS

The Red Sea is surrounded by deserts on all sides. The water temperature hardly changes with the seasons—it's about 77°F (25°C) in the summer and 70°F (21°C) in the winter. Weak currents and little rainfall result in relatively little sediment making its way to the water, which explains its rare translucence. But the nutrients in these limited sediments, along with a small supply of plankton, support the ecosystem and make it one of the richest in the world. Its diversity can be traced to the corals. Corals are colonial animals that live in symbiosis with algae. The algae harness the bountiful energy of the tropical sun using photosynthesis, producing oxygen that the corals need to live. In return, the corals give the algae protection, and generate carbon dioxide and nutrients needed by the algae. Crystal-clear waters, like those of the Red Sea, are ideal for corals, as the sunlight can penetrate into the water and fuel the system. As they grow, the large limestone "skeletons" of corals create a rare, efficient ecological system. The coral reef along the Red Sea coast is host to more than a thousand fish species, 10 percent of them found nowhere else on Earth. Pictured here is a school of sergeant major fish patrolling the shallow reef table of Jackson Reef, Straits of Tiran.

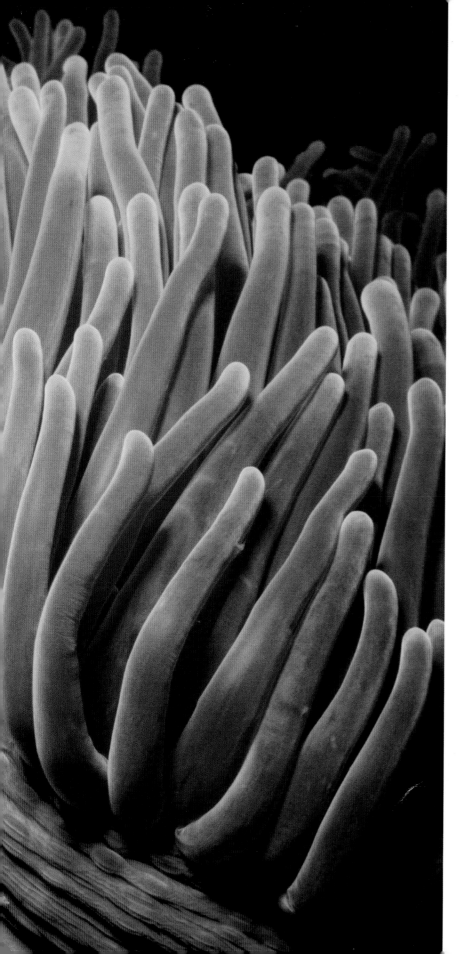

GALLERY: CAPTURING BEAUTY

Eventually, my love affair with nocturnal dives gave rise to my specialty, my unique voice (if indeed a photographer may be said to have one, particularly in that mute world): close-ups.

I'm not sure whether this "voice" was born at random or from deliberate action, and I don't think it matters. What matters is the moment in my studio when the close-ups are first laid out on the light table. In those isolated moments, I feel my subjects become disconnected from the time in which they were captured and arise in their own right, passing through my camera and onto my film with a magical touch; this is the magic where immanent secrets are revealed. It reminds me of the book *Zen in the Art of Archery*, in which the author, Eugen Herrigel, describes releasing the bowstring properly for the first time. Up to this point, he had endured countless training sessions but had yet to fire a single arrow. As the bowstring releases, he lets out a sudden whoop of delight. The master watching him says, "You are entirely innocent of this shot."

If my photographs have anything to do with art, it is only through those isolated moments when I feel completely innocent of the images I have captured. I merely provided the technology needed to seize the beauty.

When I published my close-up photos, I titled them "Fish Faces," "Fish Scales," and "Fish Tails." To me, these titles were ironic in that they shed light on the dissonance in which the parts are greater than the sum of the whole.

Magnificent sea anemone, Sipadan Island, Borneo This killing beauty's tentacles are covered with poisonous, microscopic stinging cells that will paralyze any small fish careless enough to brush up against them.

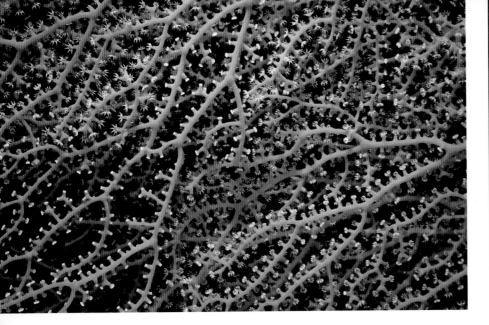

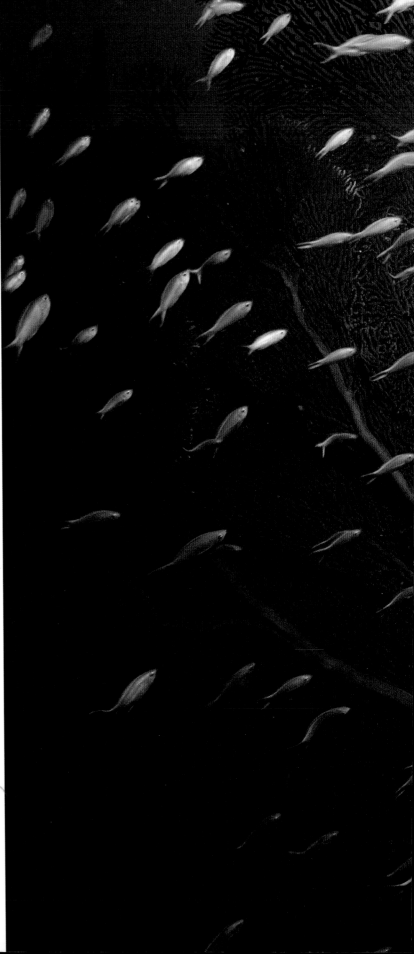

Deep-water gorgonian coral, Red Sea, Egypt This species has polyps which catch plankton and particulate matter that is consumed. The "fan" of the gorgonian is oriented across the prevailing current to increase water flow and hence food supply. (top left)

Prickly alcyonarian, Sinai Peninsula, Egypt Unlike their hard and "true" coral cousins, this species lacks the symbiotic algae which is responsible for photosynthesis; that is why alcyonarian are not restricted to sunlit spots on the reef and can grow deep. (bottom left)

Purple anthias, Kimbe Bay, Papua New Guinea This school of fish stays close to the reef, ready to dart into the protection of the nearby knotty gorgonian coral at the slightest sign of danger. Their home turf is perhaps only 10 square yards; they will not venture out farther than this. (right)

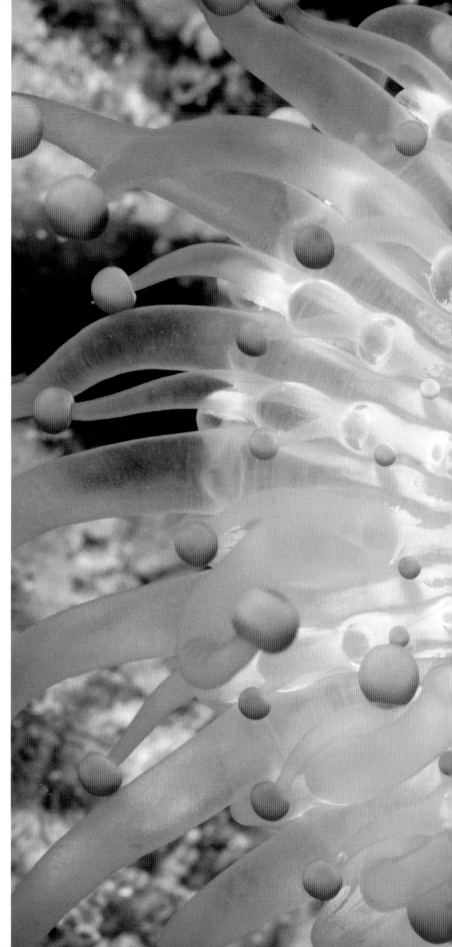

Scarlet psolus sea cucumber, Bay of Fundy, Canada This leathery invertebrate has no brain but does have a healthy appetite; it thrusts each of its ten branching tentacles into its mouth to be "licked" clean of captured plankton and organic matter. I watched the full cycle for twenty minutes, then it began all over again. (top left)

Crinoid, Kimbe Bay, Papua New Guinea This creature is a striking and unusual relative of the more familiar starfish and sea urchins. The smaller, more ropelike arms visible in this photo are used for "walking" over or grasping onto coral formations. (bottom left)

Orange ball corallimorph anemone, Grand Cayman Island (right)

Tubastrea cup coral, Sinai Peninsula, Egypt Pumped full of water and expanded to feed, these hard coral polyps will retract into their calcium carbonate skeletons at sunrise. Since they don't require the sunlight that other corals harboring algae do, they can feed at night and retreat to safety during the day. (left)

Brittle star, Sipidan Island, Borneo This creature scuttles across Alcynarian soft coral at night, coming out to scavenge under the cover of darkness. (top right)

Colonial anemone, Sinai Peninsula, Egypt (center right)

Moon jellyfish, British Columbia, Canada A juvenile, the size of my thumbnail, photographed in the frigid waters of the Queen Charlotte Straits in the North Pacific Ocean. (bottom right)

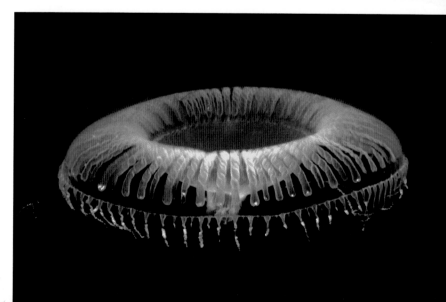

Coralline sculpin, San Clemente Island, Calif. Camouflage helps this creature hide not only from other predatory fish but also from birds.

Demon stinger, Lembeh Straight, Sulawesi, Indonesia This amazingly colored and textured member of the scorpionfish family can inject a very strong toxin through its dorsal spines. (upper left)

Red hermit crab, Ustica Island, Sicily As a hermit crab grows, it abandons its shell in search of a larger one to call home. (lower left)

Bat stars, San Clemente Island, Calif. Foraging on the holdfast of a giant kelp plant. (upper right)

Hermit crab, Lembeh Strait, Sulawesi, Indonesia Peering wearily at a gigantic photographer. (lower right)

Green turtles, Sipadan Island, Borneo
Mating underwater in cave. (left)

Moray eels, Malpelo Island, Colombia
A group hides in wait to ambush prey.
(top right)

Crown-of-thorns starfish, Red Sea, Egypt
This starfish, showing extended tubed feet
and poison spines on its arms, feeds on
coral. (center right)

Hermit crab, Red Sea, Egypt Sitting on fire
coral, out scavenging at night under cover of
darkness. (bottom right)

False clownfish and magnificent sea anemone, Papua New Guinea The clownfish, covered by special protective mucus, seeks protection in the poisonous tentacles of the sea anemone. In return, the clownfish picks it clean of parasites. Symbiosis like this is common in the ocean and can lead to some unlikely friendships between species. (top left)

Steepheaded parrotfish, Red Sea, Egypt (bottom left)

Orangespine unicornfish, Sinai Peninsula, Egypt (above)

Black triggerfish, Cocos Island, Costa Rica Its leathery mouth allows it to eat sea urchins without fear. (above)

Jewel grouper, Red Sea, Egypt (top right)

Moray eel, Eilat, Israel Even though the moray eats fish, it wouldn't dream of having these guests for dinner; the cleaner-fish go right inside its mouth to pick parasites from its teeth. (bottom right)

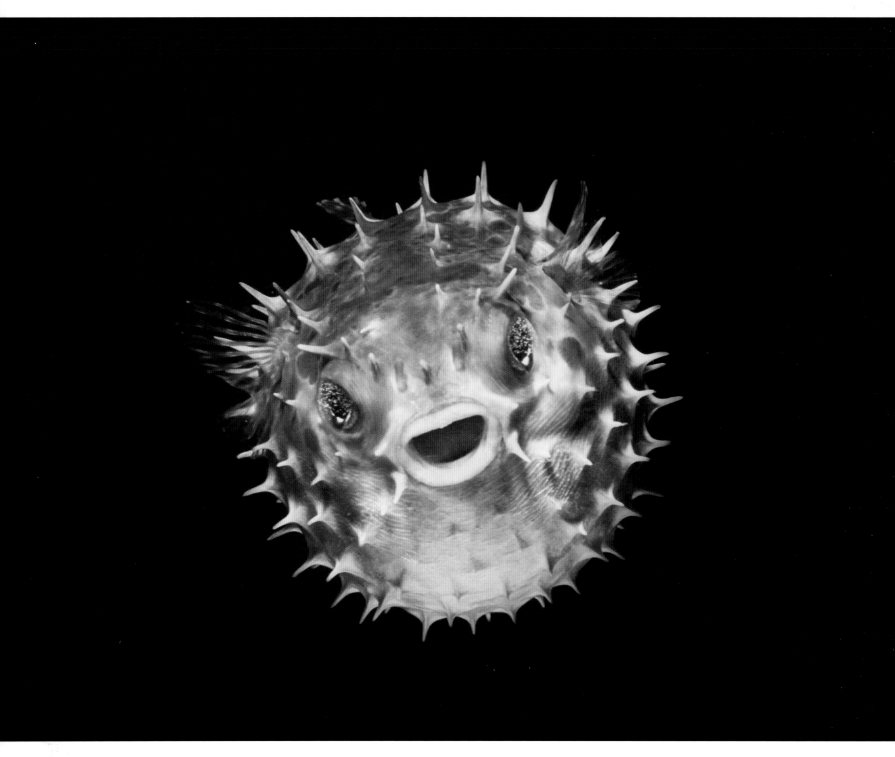

Short-spined porcupinefish, Lembeh Strait, Sulawesi, Indonesia

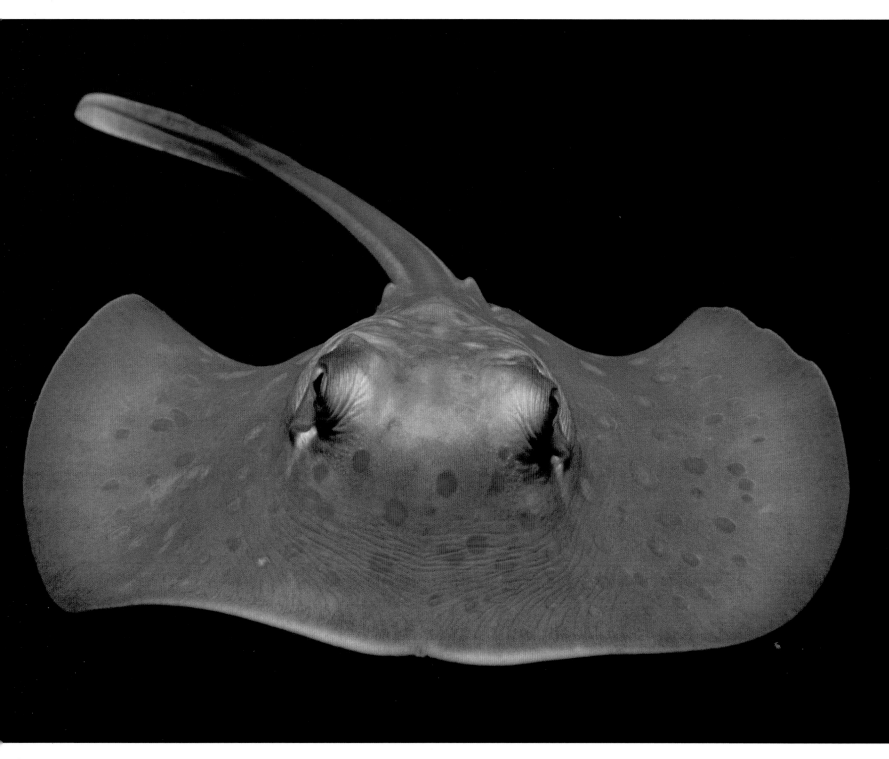

Bluespotted ribbontail stingray, Perth, Australia To me, this ray encapsulates the beauty of its species: its light blue spots look electric under the strobe light.

Tube anemone, Lembeh Strait, Sulawesi, Indonesia
Tentacles extend to sting and catch plankton in the current at night.

Hairy frogfish, Lembeh Strait, Sulawesi, Indonesia
This fish can swallow prey its own size—usually other fish, but sometimes even its own kind.

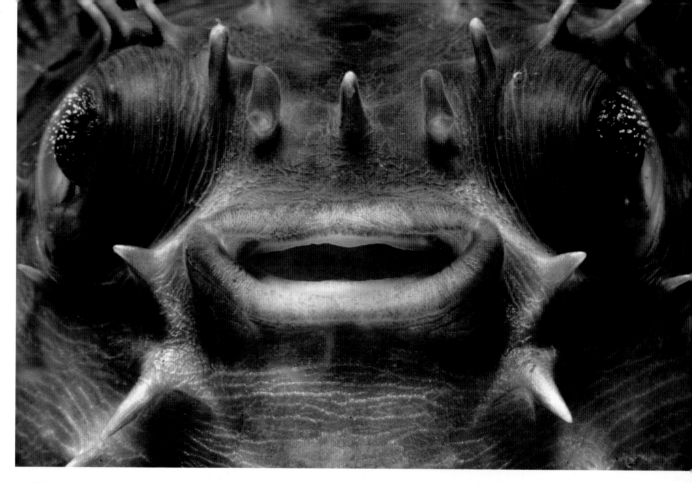

Mouth of short-spined porcupinefish, Lembeh Strait, Sulawesi, Indonesia

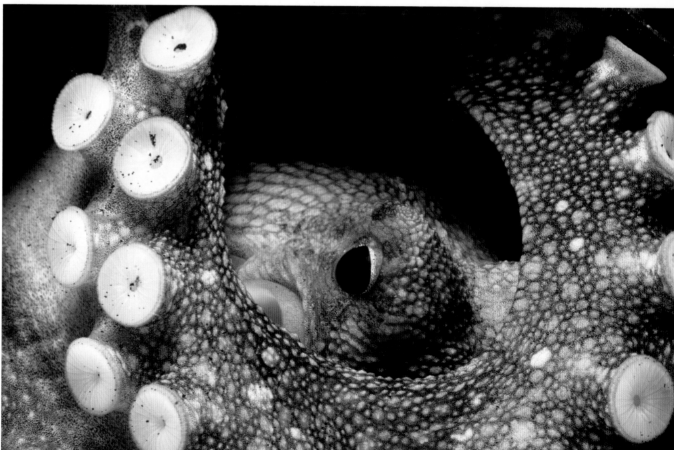

Coconut octopus, Lembeh Strait, Sulawesi, Indonesia

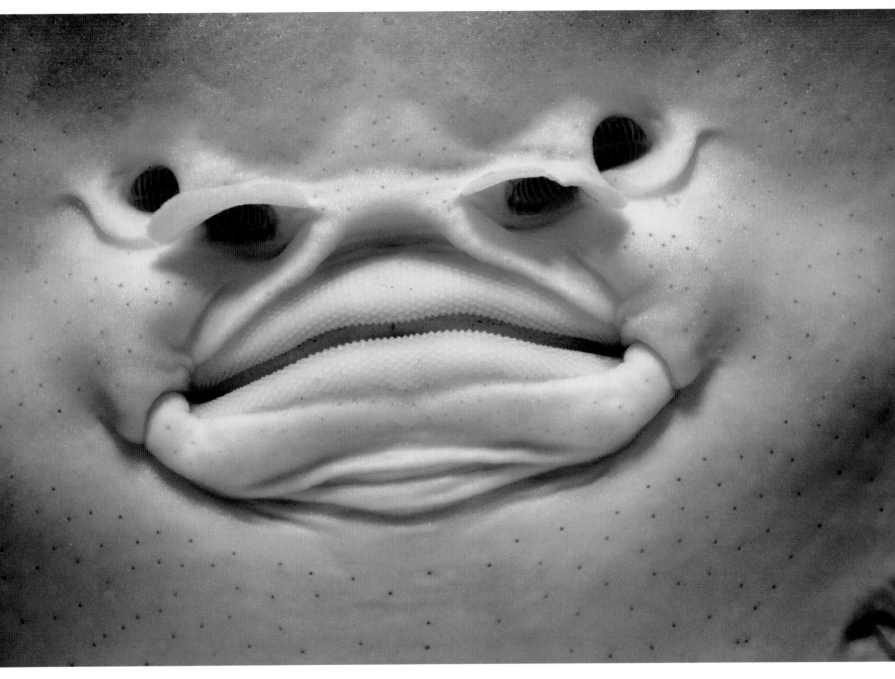

Mouth of a thornback ray, Santa Cruz Island, Calif. Its tiny grinding teeth can grip a crab before crushing the shell to devour the meat inside. This ray literally pukes its guts out—its stomach comes out of its mouth, then retracts—if it swallows something disageeable.

Anemone with a symbiotic shrimp, Sinai Peninsula, Egypt Perched on the living ledge of its host anemone, a tiny, transparent anemone shrimp eyes the camera. In yet another example of a mutually symbiotic ocean relationship, the anemone is covered with poisonous stinging cells, to which the shrimp is conveniently immune, providing a safe home for what many residents of the reef would consider a gourmet treat. In return for these lush accommodations, the shrimp keeps the host anemone clean. While they prefer their namesake, anemone shrimp have been known to form similar symbiotic relationships with other species, like mushroom coral. (1991 Underwater Wildlife Photograph of the Year, as chosen by *BBC Wildlife* magazine and the Natural History Museum of Britain)

Bigeye fish, Sinai Peninsula, Egypt (upper left)

Small-tooth grouper, Great Barrier Reef, Australia (upper right)

Queen angelfish, Freeport, Bahamas (lower left)

Squaretail grouper, Sinai Peninsula, Egypt (lower right)

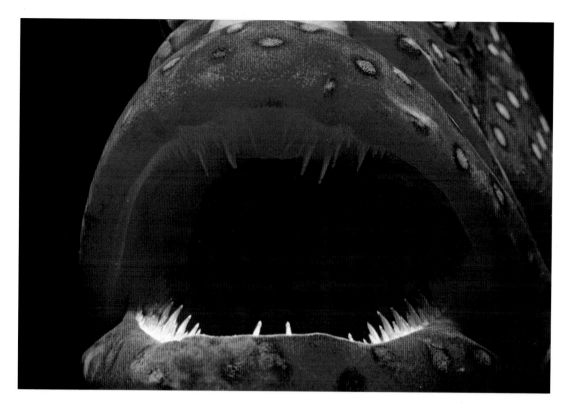

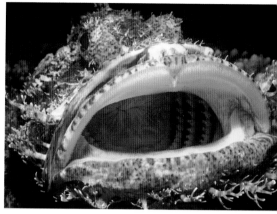

Coral grouper, Sinai Peninsula, Egypt (upper left)

Bearded scorpionfish, Brothers Islands, Red Sea, Egypt (upper right)

Deep-sea barracuda, Gulf of Eilat, Israel (bottom left)

Garibaldi, Santa Catalina Island, Calif. (middle right)

Needlefish, Sinai Peninsula, Egypt (bottom right)

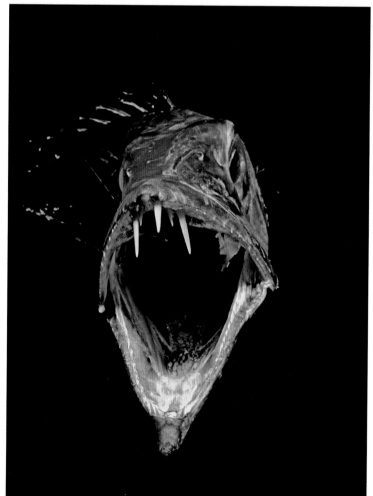

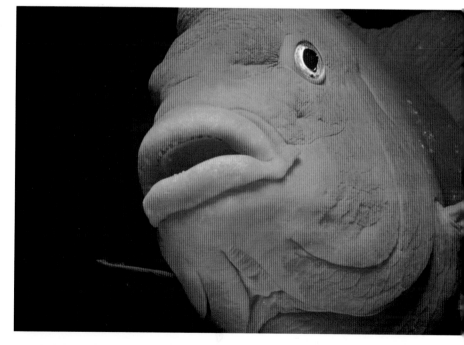

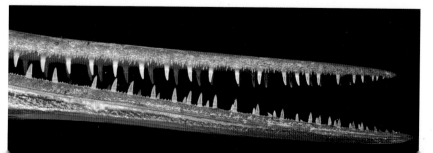

Wolf eel (wolffish), Queen Charlotte Strait, British Columbia, Canada The fish bites into a spined sea urchin. Its leathery mouth enables it to eat prickly food. (top left)

A mated pair of wolf eels, Queen Charlotte Strait, British Columbia, Canada These fish mate for life. (bottom left)

Arabian stonefish, Eilat, Israel This is the most poisonous fish on the planet, literally still as a stone with a ragged skin that strongly resembles seaweed— a perfect camouflage. (opposite, top left)

Two-stick stingfish, Eilat, Israel This species of scorpionfish uses the two sticklike protrusions on its fins to literally walk across the ocean floor, giving it its other name: "the Red Sea Walkman." (opposite, top right)

Marbled stargazer, Lembeh Straight, Sulawesi, Indonesia Lying camouflaged on a volcanic sand bottom. (opposite, bottom left)

Arabian stonefish, Eilat, Israel (opposite, bottom right)

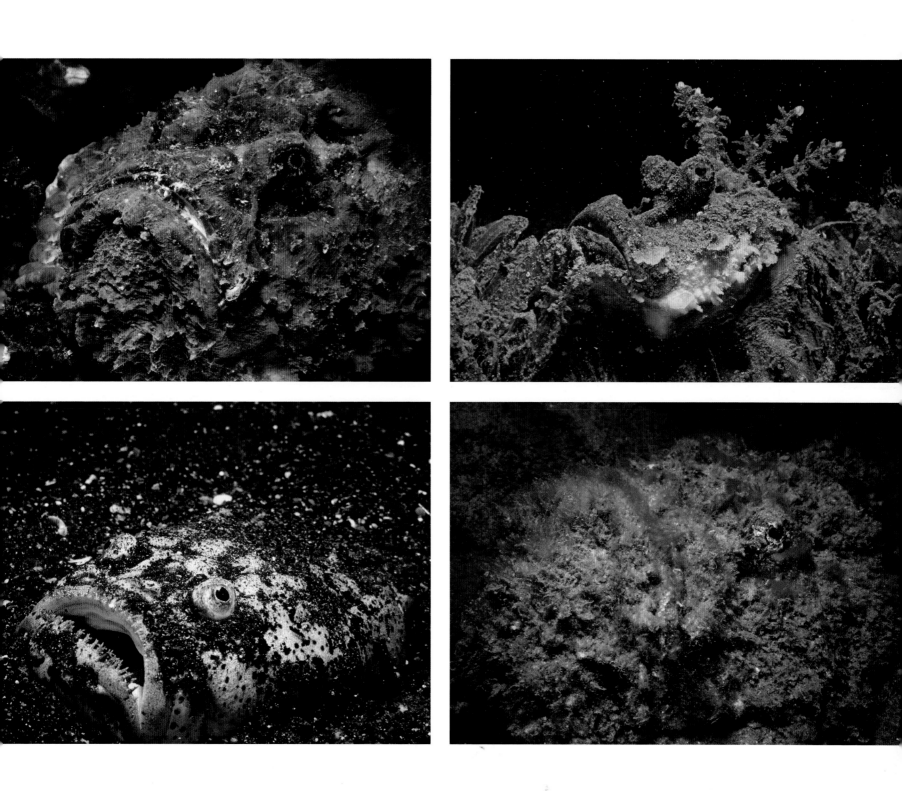

Dorsal fin of a hogfish, Bahamas
Coloration and fin modifications are used not only to warn or protect, but also to help in mate selection. (left)

Tail of a queen angelfish, Freeport, Bahamas (opposite, top)

Tail of a stoplight parrotfish, Freeport, Bahamas Konrad Lorentz, an Austrian scholar of animal behavior, described the beautiful colors and designs on fish as "poster colors" that serve the same purpose as advertising billboards—defense, mate selection, recognition, and more. (opposite, bottom)

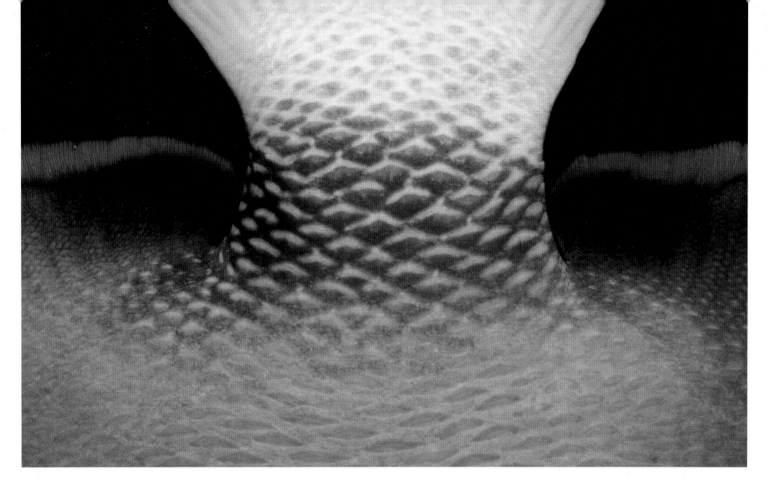

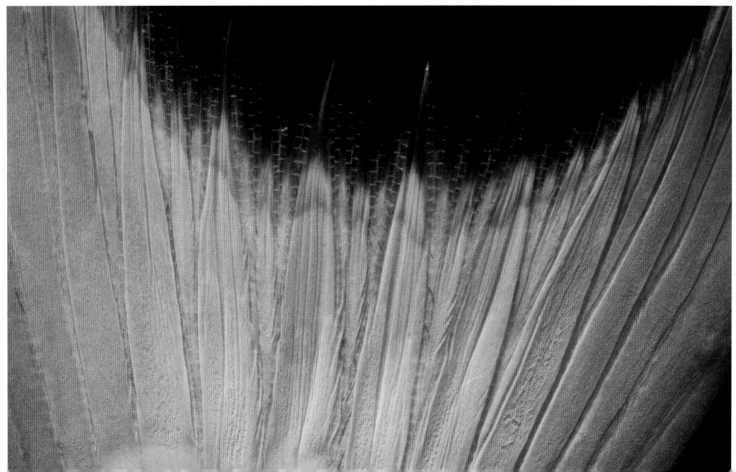

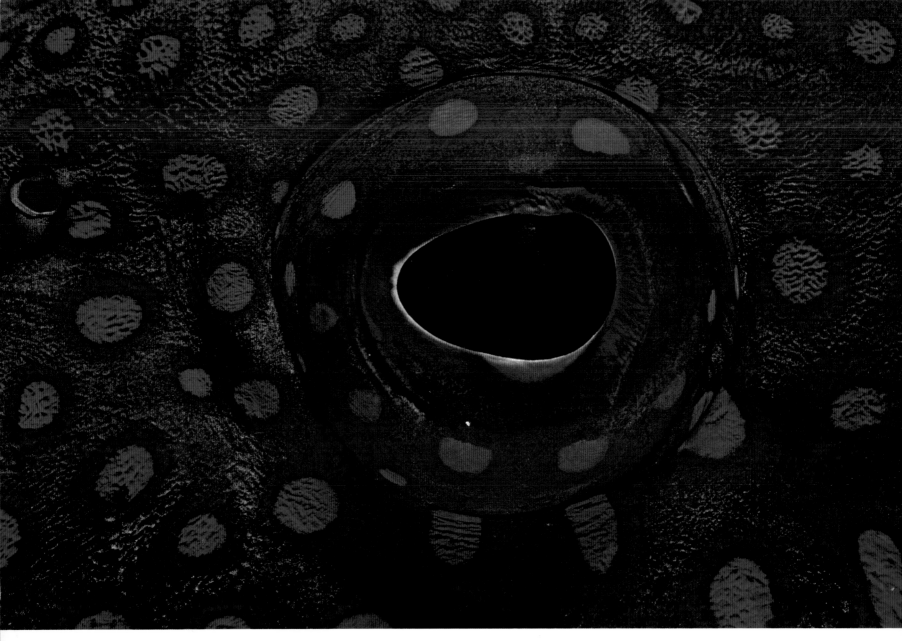

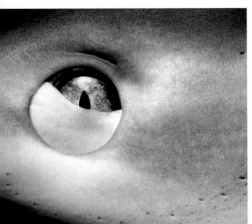

Coral grouper, Tiran Island, Egypt Fish eyes are visual feasts in and of themselves. Although it may look as though this fish has an eyelid, it cannot close it for protection like humans can. (above)

Eye of a Caribbean reef shark, Andros Island, Bahamas Nictitating membrane half closed. (far left)

Bigeye, Sinai Peninsula, Egypt (left)

Bicolor parrotfish, Sinai Peninsula, Egypt A single species of parrotfish may have four different color patterns, depending on the individual's sex and sexual maturity. Parrotfish born male will always be males, but those born female can change into males, changing colors accordingly. (opposite, top)

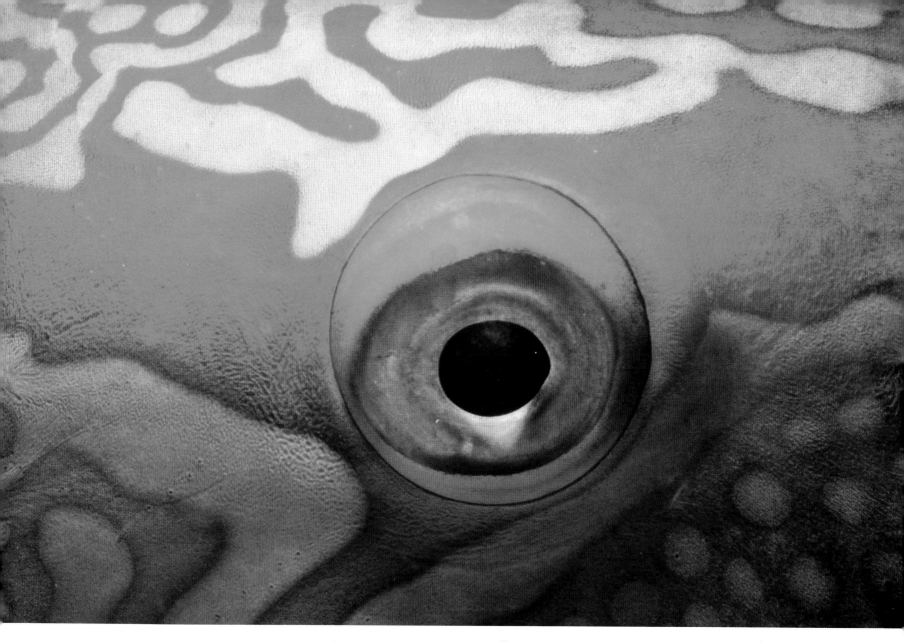

Eye of steepheaded parrotfish, Brothers Islands, Red Sea, Egypt (left)

Eye of yellow jack, Andros Island, Bahamas (right)

(page 116–117, left to right, top to bottom)
Dorsal fin of orangespine unicornfish, Red Sea, Egypt

Dorsal fin of sabre squirrelfish, Brothers Islands, Red Sea, Egypt

Pectoral fin of sohal surgeonfish, Red Sea, Egypt

Tail of rainbow parrotfish, Andros Island, Bahamas, Caribbean Sea

Dorsal fin of blackspotted sweetlips fish, Red Sea, Egypt

Pectoral fin of steepheaded parrotfish, Sinai, Red Sea, Egypt

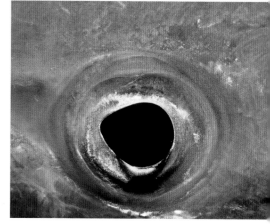

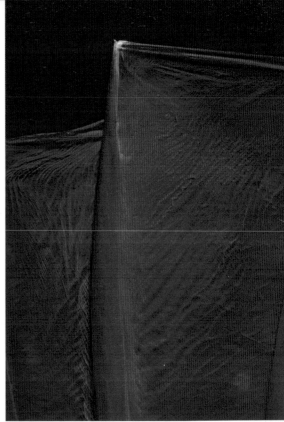

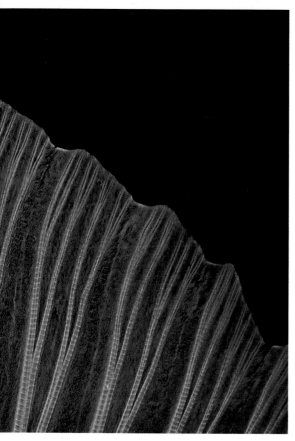

Bicolor parrotfish, Sinai Peninsula, Egypt Parrotfish eat corals, digest, and then expel them as sand. Large parrotfish can produce up to a ton of soft, white sand a year. So when tanning on a beautiful tropical sandy beach, we actually lie on parrotfish poop.

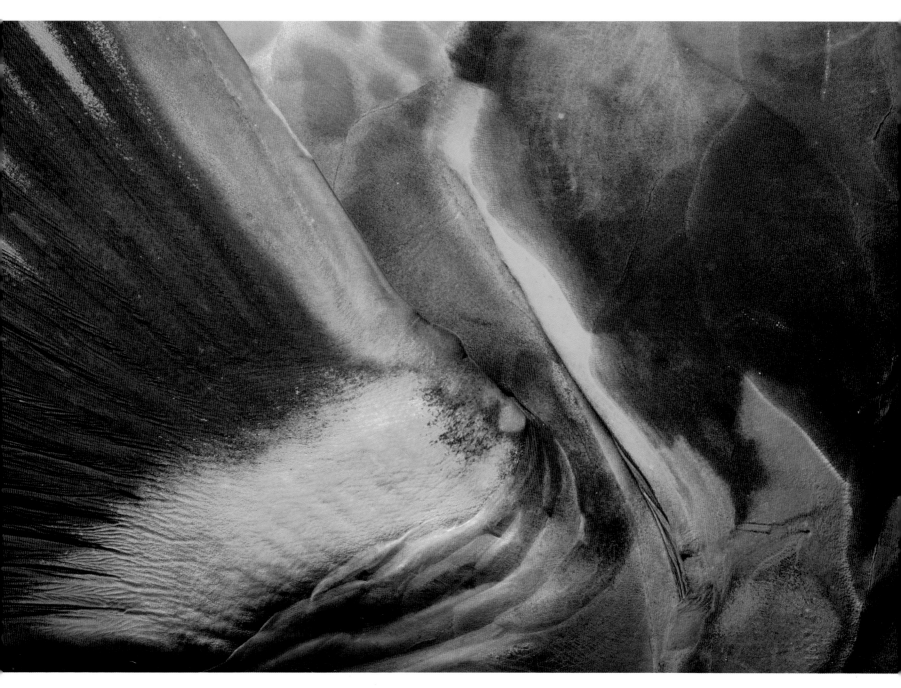

Steepheaded parrotfish, Sinai Peninsula, Egypt The many folds of a fish's gills increase the surface area over which water can flow. It flows in the opposite direction of the blood so that oxygen is constantly being passed from the water and absorbed into the blood.

SHARK
FRENZY

CLOSE ENCOUNTERS

The first time I entered shark-infested water, the familiar *daah-dum* from *Jaws* echoed in my ears, magnified by all the stories I've heard, and underlain by the bass line of my own heartbeat. Both this familiar music and the photograph I took reflect the power of sharklore and evoke the same primordial, mythic image—white jaws, seemingly disembodied, emerging out of the darkness, crowned by a nose as focused and intent as an arrow shot by a master archer, pointed toward the target by narrow, evil eyes.

In the timeless sky of my memories, this photograph shimmered as if it were already a piece of tangible reality—even before I entered the water. In fact, I have found that when it comes to sharks, my experiences live side by side in my memory, resistant to chronology and thereby retaining their primal nature. Time after time, whenever I recall an experience I've had with a shark, or many sharks, it is as if I am right back there, experiencing it for the first time.

Sand tiger shark, N.C. If looks can kill . . . This shark is one of the best candidates to help dispel this myth. Its "look from hell" is not a show of aggression, but rather a typical shark behavior known as . . . yawning. Actually, sand tiger sharks are a very shy species.

Close Encounter of the First Kind

I dove into the Ras Muhammad coral reef at the southern tip of the Sinai Peninsula. In those days, you could still meet the huge predators before waves of tourists swarmed the reef and scared them away. I dove on my own, prepared for the encounter. I knew they were there and was well aware of their tendency to sneak up on the unguarded. I sat on a ledge with my back to the reef, protected from that side—or so I thought. I prepared the camera, my eye locked on the viewfinder, my finger on the trigger, and waited. I was ready to capture the moment.

I find it very difficult to stay focused when I am idle. Waiting for the sharks, I was both doing and hearing nothing. I needed to stay engaged in an activity, even a monotonous one. So I tried to regulate the noise of the bubbles I was making. I hoped that even a cautious shark would become used to the rhythm and eventually ignore it. I couldn't ignore it, however: For one waiting underwater, the sound made by the bubbles marks a countdown to asphyxiation.

And then, there it was—just about one meter away. A hammerhead shark. It was as though the mystery of the submarine myths was revealed to me through its most outlandish manifestation. It emerged out of a blind spot at the edge of my mask and then turned in an upward sweep. I released the shutter at just the right moment, my flash painting a tiny bit of light on the shark to bring out the color. The hammerhead disappeared in an instant. But I could still feel it, from all directions at once, as if we were wrapped together in the flash-lit water.

I knew I had captured a *perfect* image on film. I knew because I was looking through the viewfinder when I took the photo, and as the flash went off, I could see the frozen frame. I had been looking for such an image ever since I started diving eight years earlier, and now I had it.

Over the course of my career, I have taken thousands of shark photos, but all those I have successfully captured are mirrored by all those I have missed. The ones that came out well (some even pretty well, if I do say so myself) are locked in their frames, visible and well formed, permanent keepsakes. But those I have missed are still alive and kicking, taunting me with their freedom, taking on the volume of a timeless story. All of these missed opportunities haunt my dreams, but none so much as that first shark—the hammerhead. In my dream he swims toward then away from me slowly, retracing his underwater fish-steps as if knowing what was about to happen, showing off his beauty and his power. Crossing my frame once again, he practically poses for my camera, and then finally withdraws, waving his tail goodbye.

Back on land, as I went to rewind the film, the terrible truth hit me: The film had never caught on the sprockets when I loaded it into the camera. I had taken my "once in a lifetime" photo of nothing.

Scalloped hammerhead, Kaneohe Bay, Hawaii There is no mistaking a hammerhead shark; its broad, flat head looks like it has been squeezed in a vise. Widely spaced eyes and nostrils might make these sharks' senses more acute; they might also add lift and improve swimming efficiency.

Whitetip reef sharks, Cocos Island, Costa Rica Cruising the reefs like a pack of wolves coming out to hunt, these sharks lie still for long stretches on sandy bottoms, dispelling the common myth that all sharks must constantly swim to breathe. Whitetip sharks actively pump water over their gills to keep oxygen flowing.

Second First Time

Moonless night. Ernst Meier and I went into the water to shoot a moray eel in its lair, which we had discovered that morning. We took some fish as bait and strapped them to our waists on fishing lines. We floated over the water for last-minute preparations and joked about how many fingers we were willing to lose for a good shot while feeding these creatures. Then we released the air out of the buoyancy compensators and started our descent.

A different guest had invited itself to our dinner party with the eels, however. The minute I turned on my flashlight to start the search, I saw it—a whitetip reef shark, looking just as shocked as I was. The first beam, shooting across the darkness and hitting it like lightning, seemed to deliver it a powerful jolt. It became frenzied, as if smelling a victim's blood. I shook the flashlight wildly to warn Ernst and he turned his own light toward the shark, which had disappeared for a moment but left the water heavily charged with its ominous presence.

I moved back toward Ernst, and we clung to each other and lit the water together. The shark reappeared, moving swiftly towards us, then made an abrupt U-turn and disappeared momentarily. It crossed our light ray again—from right to left and back. I pulled on Ernst's arm and shone my light onto his face. We understood each other perfectly. He pointed with his flashlight to the inevitable conclusion: Up! Out! Now!

We swam quickly to the reef table, knelt on our knees and took our heads out of the water. I don't remember if we burst out laughing right away or after several anxious moments. Ernst spread his hands to indicate a length not much bigger than the size of his chest and muttered mockingly, "No more than two feet! That's what one tiny, shy shark can do to two giant men."

In the spirit of Ernst's mocking gesture and in opposition to virtually all sharks encountered by divers (including me), the size of this shark keeps *shrinking* as this story is retold year after year.

Juvenile whitetip reef shark, Cocos Island On this particular dive, Asher and I encountered—and solved—a bit of a mystery. Although we were surrounded by many whitetip reef sharks, there were no juveniles in sight. Then, in a cave about 50 feet down, we found five juvenile whitetips lying on top of each other.

Close Encounter with the Supreme

Adding to the value of the photos that were to follow, my private shark mythology includes yet another failure. This one occurred during my first encounter with the meanest, purest evil—the great white shark.

Stan Waterman, often regarded as the American Jacques Cousteau, invited me to the southern Australian coast to dive. He warned me that the journey, which required a considerable investment of both time and resources, came with no guarantees—his experience had taught him never to promise results when it came to great whites. But I trusted my good fortune, especially since I was accompanied by the man who played himself in *The Man Who Loves Sharks*. How could the sharks resist us?

Two years earlier I had collaborated with Stan on a project together with the man responsible, perhaps more than any other, for the modern shark myth—Peter Benchley, the author of *Jaws*. We were taking photographs off the California coast to illustrate the destructive impact fishing had on the blue shark population. We had low expectations when we got to the site and started to "chum in" (diver jargon for baiting sharks with blood and strong-smelling, oily mackerel). We were hoping for maybe one or two sharks. Just the opposite happened. I guess when the sharks (tens of them) heard that Stan and Peter were in attendance, they just couldn't resist making an appearance.

Now, in Australia, Stan and I were joined by yet another shark guru, the (barely) living legend, Rodney Fox. Rodney survived a great white shark attack that necessitated 462 stitches to sew him back together. I imagined his scars as I watched Rodney ladle a smelly mixture of outdated human blood, rancid tuna, and very ripe horse meat into the water, creating a chum slick that would hopefully bring in the "white death."

And it did. It took several long days of waiting in the cage (exactly how many I have since forgotten), but eventually one showed up—a dark, blurry stain, like the shadow of a body momentarily blocking out the sun. It swam toward us, then dove deep. I was prepared for it, ready even for its way of surprising its prey. A mighty wave shook the cage when it ascended directly out of the blind spot below us, revealing itself to us in its full glory.

A safety diver wearing a chain mail suit being bitten by a blue shark San Clemente Island, Calif. (top)

Rodney Fox Perhaps the most famous shark attack victim, Fox holds up photo-graphs that seem to become parts of his body, strengthened and hardened over years of recounting his story and relentlessly pursuing his nemesis: the great white. (bottom)

In full view of the cage, the shark twice drew back a little and then returned, sizing us up with the discriminating eyes of a connoisseur whose taste has been evolving over a period of sixty-five million years. I was mesmerized. When I awoke from my hypnotic trance—the minute he was gone—I realized that I hadn't taken a single shot.

For a brief moment, there in the cage in the presence of the shark, I had been elated, even proud. It was as if all the preparations and resources invested up to this point were a worthy sacrifice for that single, priceless moment. Of course, by the time I got back to the boat, I was cursing that elation and pride, cursing my whole day. In terms of results, it was as anticlimactic as they came.

Great white shark, Dangerous Reef, South Australia Nothing can prepare you for this wonder—not stories that you've heard, nor films you've seen on the big or small screen, not even rigorous mental preparation and the expectation. Surprise!

IN SEARCH OF BEAUTY AND AWE: SHARK FRENZY

But eventually I got a second opportunity, and a more generous one at that, to photograph "Mister Big" (as we called each one of our favorite guests) during that voyage. Five great whites appeared before us, together and separately, over eight consecutive days, and those times, I managed to find my shutter finger.

Who's Afraid of the Big Bad Fish?

People who look at my idyllic photos of colorful fish floating over the reef often ask me, "How do you avoid sharks?" I tell them that the best anti-shark device I have come across is an underwater photographer with a fully loaded camera looking to take photographs of sharks. Then I lecture, to anyone who wants to listen, on everything I know about the fish: that they are shy, are the crowning glory of evolution, are not all the same (there are many different types of sharks), and so on. I often find it hard to explain my attraction to these creatures, lodged somewhere in my mind between primordial fear and theoretical knowledge. This tension underlies my obsession to "get" sharks, to understand these ancient mariners and their underwater ways.

Photographing sharks is a challenge, as they are cautious creatures groomed over eons of evolutionary time to know their enemies and carefully choose their prey. Even the notorious "man-eaters" would rather avoid any encounter with us, the unwelcome invasive species that has crept into all corners of the sharks' domain. These masters of the fathoms are not attracted to the strange and giant creatures we become underwater, with our armors of rubber and metal, and bodies whose volume (including the bubbles we emit) reaches up to the water's surface. Thus, to capture sharks on film, one must either rely on fortuitous, fleeting encounters or lure them closer with enticements, daring them to take risk for a culinary reward.

Over time, I have learned to recognize and classify sharks into their different species. To obtain optimal results, I have had to focus on a specific species each dive trip, getting to know it well: its favorite prey, its seasonal migratory habits, its customary depths, and other characteristics. Sometimes, during my observations, I discovered things I hadn't previously known.

One such occasion occurred when I was three hundred miles off the Costa Rican coast, diving off Cocos Island (the "Island of the Sharks"). Every day at approximately 4PM, four to six silvertip sharks would appear at a particular rock outcrop at the depth of about 33 feet (10 meters) where a

Great white, Dangerous Reef, South Australia Even from within the relative safety of an anti-shark cage, Mr. Big made me feel as if he were burning me into his memory for the next time we met eye-to-eye. (opposite)

Great whites Coal-black eyes and gleaming white teeth are the images forever remembered by people who have encountered a great white shark face-to-face. (above)

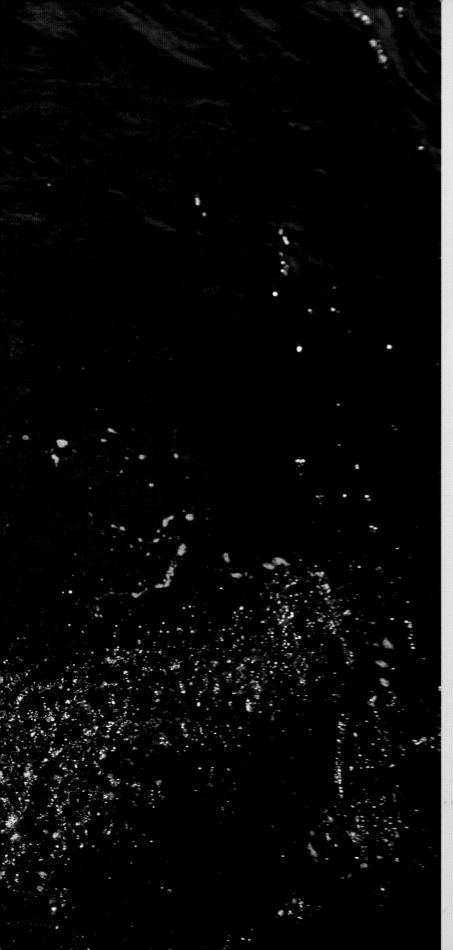

THIRTY-FOUR DAYS FOR ONE MOMENT

It's very hard to plan for a shot in natural history photography. This particular shot, however, had been carefully planned because I knew exactly what I wanted.

Again, I traveled to the other end of the globe, this time to South Africa. There was a man there, Andre Hartman, who had become famous for his ability to chum the great white to the dive platform on the back of his boat, and then, just as it got within reach, pull the bait out of the water and touch the great white's nose. This triggered a reflex reaction: The great white would open its horrible maw wide and show you its teeth—a spectacular shot. But you needed just the right conditions for this to happen: a flat, oily, calm sea.

I counted the days. Thirty-four. It took thirty-four days before I got my few seconds of opportunity. I finally had my chance.

It was worth it.

small school of juvenile trevally jacks lived. Each day, the silvertips would swim toward the end of the outcrop and then slow down so that the smaller trevallys could clean them: a silvertip "cleaning station." This behavior—removal of parasites from the fish's body—is common to many different types of fish, but to my knowledge at the time, had never before been observed with silvertips.

Silvertips are one of very few shark species that have a reputation for being aggressive toward divers, and therefore should be approached with caution. I dove to the depth of the cleaning station, but to a spot horizontally about 16 feet (5 meters) away. Then I had my safety diver, Asher Gal, hang back and wait behind me as I slowly approached. I took approximately thirty minutes to cover the 16 feet. I used this time to practice skip breathing, which means breathing as slowly and shallowly as possible to minimize the sound and quantity of released air bubbles that could scare the sharks. Skip breathing can be effective, but it is also dangerous—in fact, some divers pass out from it.

This is one of the problems with underwater photography. On a dive, because of the limited air, a diver cannot wait endlessly for the subjects to appear or to act. Neither can he use telescopic lenses to compensate for his own visibility and the sound he makes, which can deter the animal from getting close.

I returned to the cleaning station eight days in a row, spending a total of about two hours each time just beneath the action. I knew I was witnessing something extraordinary.

No matter how many discoveries are made, ultimately, our knowledge is still limited. We must never underestimate the capabilities of the creatures we encounter, nor should we ever overestimate our own. Asher once learned this painful (almost literally) lesson when he rushed to save me from a big tiger shark that was making an open-mouthed approach. Displaying some combination of superb instinct and momentary madness, Asher grabbed the shark's tail. With amazing flexibility, the beast arched its entire body back toward its tail. Asher later swore that he heard its jaws snapping shut only inches from his fingers.

Silvertip shark, Cocos Island, Costa Rica As I approached this particularly aggressive shark, I almost released a bubble of laughter when the famous scene from *The Good, the Bad and the Ugly* popped into my head. Out of its intimate position in his "bath," this shark could draw his gun on me. So I shot first.

In this environment, you cannot exaggerate the importance of expecting the unexpected. Divers are not the only ones to embrace this wisdom—the sharks themselves seem to survive thanks to that wisdom. I once had the dubious fortune of witnessing sharks exhibit their own keen awareness and ability to swiftly respond to their environment.

On this particular occasion, I was in mid-ocean, diving among some thirty Caribbean reef sharks. I was shooting them as they circled around me, presenting a variety of angles and postures, when, without any warning, they all scattered and disappeared. There could have been only one reason for this sudden exodus, and indeed, I soon felt its presence. A huge hammerhead, at least 20 feet (6 meters) in length, was approaching me from behind. My back is usually covered by Asher, but my guardian angel was not with me. Nor, as I was in the open ocean, was there any nearby reef to offer protection. There was nothing I could do but rely on the shark's discriminating taste. He crossed the water in front of me. His eyes locked on mine. But he cruised on and away from my trembling limbs without looking back.

Tiger shark, Red Sea Although I was the hero of a TV crew who came to film a story about *The Man Who Loves Sharks*, Asher is the true hero of this picture. When this shark came in for the kill, Asher grabbed the beast by the tail. The shark whipped around to bite and barely missed Asher's unprotected hands.

BASKING SHARK

Basking sharks are amazing and beautiful creatures, a special beast in every way. Trying to photograph them off the Isle of Man in the middle of the Irish Sea was one of the most frustrating experiences I've ever had. I went to work with a scientist who was trying to put satellite tags on a few specimens, and the Isle of Man is one of the few places where they can be found during the summer months. They go there to feast on a seasonal plankton upwelling which, as you might surmise, made visibility close to impossible. Adding to that, it rains almost constantly, which limits available light, and the animal is too large to illuminate with a strobe. To make the enterprise even more challenging, the water was frigid, and I had to take the shots free-diving because basking sharks scare easily, becoming frightened at the slightest disturbance like bubbles coming up from my tank. I had to go two summers in a row to get a good shot. It took that long to conquer all of the pitfalls of the conditions: low visibility, poor weather, skittish sharks frightened into deep dives, or missing sharks altogether. (When the plankton weren't the type the shark fed on, they would amuse themselves elsewhere.) But I did get the shot in the end.

WHALE SHARK

We used a spotter plane to find this beautiful animal off the Ningaloo Reef on the Western Australia shoreline. On the fourth day of trying, we struck gold, sighting the first of many whale sharks we would see in the course of our trip. I dove in. Whale sharks are the biggest of all fish, and I had never seen one in all my years of diving. The creature's amazing size and docility did not disappoint. As it swam by, I grabbed its dorsal fin with one hand and kept shooting with my other hand. This is the advantage of using a simple, tiny camera like the Nikonos with its sharp-as-can-be 15 mm lens. I was using a tiny pony air tank and, when the shark and I reached 130 feet (40 meters), I started to run out of air. I barely made it back to the surface, but what a ride! Two days later I tried the trick again with another whale shark, but it was moving too fast and I wasn't able to grasp its dorsal fin. I tried grabbing the tail—and almost got whacked into the next ocean when it let me know that I was a weak and unwelcome guest in its world.

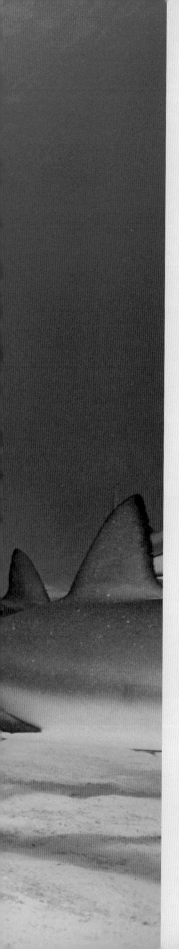

UNDERWATER KNIGHTS

In nature photography, the border between neutral observer, patiently waiting for the perfect shot to materialize, and participant, actively affecting the environment to help that shot materialize, often becomes blurred.

It has become fashionable for underwater photographers to work with feeding stations primarily established to entertain tourists. It is like a performance. Regular tourists pay one hundred dollars and are taken on a dive in a location where sharks have been conditioned to come for food. They are told to kneel down in the sand on the sea floor and keep their hands close to their bodies. Then the "feeder" appears in a full chain mail suit with a container of dead fish. Taking out these dead fish, one by one, he hand-feeds sharks, mainly reef sharks. The exhibition is conducted safely and people are so close that they could reach out and touch a shark. (They are not allowed to do this but they could—they are that close.) Not only is this arrangement a real money-making machine for those involved, but the sharks seem to enjoy it, too, showing up on cue as they hear the boat motors approach.

I also have enjoyed these stations. I would go down 50 feet (15 meters) with a feeder and Asher. On one of my first dives, I was nearly bitten when a few scraps of fish drifted on top of my thigh. On the next trip, I rented a chain mail suit. The suit was a revelation, as it allowed me to relax and totally concentrate. Although it would be useless with bigger and more powerful sharks like tigers (the power of their jaws would easily crush one's bones), Caribbean reef sharks cannot easily penetrate the chain mail. Sometimes, however, the teeth of a particularly large individual reef shark would get caught in the links and the shark would take me with it when it swam away. I'm sure it looked very comical. The action at the reef was nonstop. The sharks were so comfortable and conditioned to being fed that I might as well have been shooting goldfish swimming around in a bowl.

A group of tourists are instructed to kneel down in the sand and keep their hands close to their bodies as they watch a shark feeder with Caribbean reef sharks, Freeport, Bahamas.

The Bait Ball: The Image That Couldn't Be Taken

Not all sharks know about my nine-lives quota. Although I did have some vague idea of the thin boundary between observer and participant, I needed the next encounter to really appreciate it completely.

I waited through seven days of dives off Cocos Island for it to happen. Asher and I had come to these waters on a mission to shoot a "bait ball"—a school of fish, usually green jacks (which look like miniature tuna), sometimes numbering in the thousands, that have been herded together and forced towards the surface by hungry predators. The bait-balling technique is often practiced by sharks, dolphins, swordfish, and marlins—sometimes working together in a coalition.

I was accompanied by a guide (Peter), a Zodiac boat pilot (José), and Asher. Together, we gazed towards the horizon, searching for the telltale sign—birds flocking on the surface to join the feeding frenzy.

We had been at it for a very long week. Spending day after day staring through binoculars on the open sea from a Zodiac is enough to drive you nuts. We might have given up sooner, if the signs of action hadn't kept nibbling on the thin cord of our patience. Time and again, we would rush as fast as José could take us to the edge of the horizon where a flock of birds was spotted. But time and again, we would arrive after a long, rough boat ride to find that the vision had deluded us like a mirage, or, worse, that the birds were replete, resting on the water or taking off heavily, their stomachs full, the show over.

Whitetip reef sharks, Cocos Island Having picked up the scent of a wounded fish, a group of whitetip sharks searches frantically for the source. Some sharks' sense of smell is so keen, they can detect a drop of blood in a million drops of water. (left)

Wobbegong shark, New South Wales, Australia This shark is so confident of its efficient camouflage that it refuses to budge even when it has been discovered: a perfect opportunity for a photographer. When this shark does move—and bite—it doesn't let go. (above)

Spiny dogfish, Gloucester, Mass. This is a rare photograph of a newborn spiny dogfish shark with its yolk sac still attached. It is possible that this particular fetus was spontaneously aborted when its mother was netted by fishermen. I was told that it had no chance of survival. (opposite)

Caribbean reef shark, Walkers Cay, Bahamas A few times on night dives, my flashlight beam has triggered the eerie glow of a shark's eye caught peering at me out of the darkness. Like cats, some sharks have a light-reflective layer behind their retinas that improves their vision in dim light. (top right)

Port Jackson shark, South Australia What could be more engaging than this whimsical portrait? The shark's mouth seems to open in a winsome smile that makes you almost want to pet it. (bottom right)

Whitetip reef sharks, Cocos Island, Costa Rica Forcing their noses into a crevice in the reef and pounding like crazy with their tails, the sharks broke apart the rock where a fish was hiding. The fish was captured by one lucky shark; the others could only share the scent of blood and go berserk. (following pages)

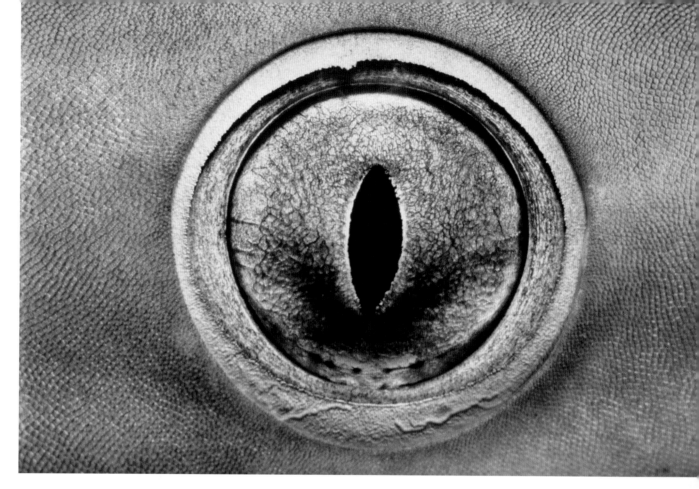

I had set a limit of seven days—lucky seven. On the seventh day, an hour and a half before our last sunset, we headed toward a flock of birds several miles from the boat. This time it was not a false alarm—the show was in full swing. We stopped the Zodiac about 330 feet (100 meters) from the site of the carnage and turned off the engine.

All hell was breaking loose. Bird squeaks tore the air around us as hundreds took off and landed in the water one after another, as in carefully timed bomber sorties. Shark fins were almost audibly slicing through the surface.

This wasn't going to be the first time we found ourselves in the eye of a storm of sharks reveling on blood and bait we had thrown to them. Having in the past grabbed the tail of a tiger shark three times his size, Asher felt confident in his ability to watch both me and himself. We thought we knew enough to weather the bait ball. Wasting no time, Asher and I jumped in with our diving and filming gear.

The squeaking and slicing fell silent. We swam toward the heart of the action. Suddenly, about 200 feet (60 meters) away from the bait ball, loud clicks and squeaks filled the water as dolphins aligned for an attack, marking the boundaries of the battlefield. Immediately afterwards, as though by cue, we saw the first shark—a silky. Out of nowhere, its friends joined it, fifty or maybe more, cutting in from all directions. We still hadn't reached the bait ball—we couldn't even see the bait ball. The sun was low and the light was dwindling.

The silkies swam near Asher and me. They were beautiful beasts with lovely coloration, soft gold lines set across shades of silver. I decided to take a picture, but because the light level was so low I was forced to use a flash. *Pop!—Pop!—Pop!* went my electronic strobe, and with each click, the strobe emitted a very high-pitched squeal as it recharged. Each squeal lasted only three seconds, but the noise drove the sharks crazy. I was fully aware of this typical reaction—but I wanted the picture!

Almost immediately the silkies started zooming in on us, pointing their pectoral fins down and arching their backs to show they meant business. Asher, who was behind me, turned me to face an approaching shark. It was just 12 inches (30 centimeters) from my face when it swerved sharply in front of my nose. It was exciting—I loved it. But then there were just too many. We could not keep track of them. All of a sudden—*thump!*—one of them plowed into my side. This was not a love tap. It felt like being punched in the kidneys by a professional boxer. We knew that this behavior is common to dolphins, and occasionally to sharks as well—we were under attack. They didn't need to bite, they just needed to punch, intent on pulverizing us with internal injuries, making us easy to "collect."

We were both approaching a state of panic. Things had gotten completely out of control. We turned and swam back toward the Zodiac as the sharks continued to have their fun. José, having seen what was happening, had started the engine and now

Tiger shark, **Coral Sea, Australia** This 15-foot-long tiger shark continuously harassed Asher Gal, my assistant of twenty-five years ("Superman, size medium," as I call him). The shark's aggression forced us to leave the water: Caution is the better part of valor.

raced toward us. As soon as he reached us, we got out of the water and rolled over the side of the boat into what we both assumed was safety. But the bait ball had followed us and was now directly under the boat. The fish, seeing the boat as shelter, stuck with us as we moved. There was no escape. For better or worse, we became the center of the action.

The scene was breathtaking. Birds sat on the surface, so stuffed with fish that they could no longer take off. Sharks swam up through the bait ball, eyes protected by nictitating membranes—a typical mechanism when feeding. They broke the surface, chomping mouths stuffed with green jacks, and rose a good foot and a half (half a meter) out of the water. Every ten seconds or so, one would slam into the Zodiac's reinforced wooden bottom in a powerful collision. After the first few of these assaults, we wondered if they might actually tear the boat apart.

Still intent on shooting despite it all, I tried to stick the camera over the side of the boat to take a picture, but it was impossible. Each time, a shark would slam into the heavy aluminum housing of the camera, unbalancing me. The water surface was boiling; I had never seen anything so surreal. Asher and I looked at each other and let out a peel of nervous, excited laughter. Professionals or not, we were in an advanced state of shock, as were Peter and José. The chaos continued for nearly thirty minutes. And then, the moment the sun dropped into the sea, as if a switch had been flipped, the ocean fell completely silent and peace reigned once again.

In my private album, I give a special honor to the one picture that was not captured. In this instance, I did not miss the shot because of a technical error, poor visibility, or some other mundane reason—it was simply a picture that could not be taken.

Scalloped hammerheads schooling in Cocos Island Hammerhead sharks always excite me. When small, like these scalloped hammerheads, they look comical, as if carrying weird surveillance instruments. But when I meet an 11-foot great hammerhead it looks downright frightening, as if carrying an efficient killing machine. (top)

Velvet belly shark, Mediterranean Sea, Haifa, Israel This full-grown shark is only about 9 inches long. Its velvet belly is bioluminescent with light-emitting photophores— organs used for attracting food and confusing predators, and which might also play a role in social interactions. (bottom)

Blue shark, San Clemente Island, Calif. (opposite)

Caribbean reef sharks, Freeport, Bahamas (right)

Caribbean reef shark, Nassau, Bahamas This shark's nictitating membrane covers and protects its eyes as the shark prepares to take a bite out of me. I, of course, had on my chain mail suit. Never leave home without it! (page 156)

Bigeye thresher shark, Cocos Island This majestic shark was more than 10 feet long. Its most startling feature is a long, curving upper tail lobe (nearly as long as the rest of the shark), which it uses to stun the pelagic fish it hunts. (page 157, top)

Caribbean reef shark, Freeport, Bahamas (page 157, center)

Sand tiger shark, New South Wales, Australia This fearsome-looking beast is a popular exhibit in public aquariums because its protruding, daggerlike teeth provide the spine-chilling thrill that visitors seek. (page 157, bottom)

THE BITE

Half a year after our bait-ball adventure, Asher and I returned to Cocos Island for another diving trip. We were out on the water with Pacheco, our new captain; in the distance, boats dotted the horizon.

All at once, the boats disappeared. Clouds had started gathering above the island and the wind was picking up, but Pacheco said the atmosphere had nothing to do with their departure. "The pirates," as he called them, must have taken off after spotting a coast guard boat. But as the hours passed, the horizon remained empty for no apparent reason. It felt menacing.

From the deck, we could see the shores of Cocos Island, known for legendary treasure hoards of historic pirates, and, more recently, famed for what have become rare natural treasures, mainly sharks. Sharks abound in these waters in all species and sizes, attracting two special kinds of tourists: divers like me, and what the captain calls "pirates"—nothing more than longline fishermen.

Maybe because of their sudden disappearance, and maybe because of the pejorative nickname given to them by the captain, my curiosity was piqued. In the middle of my expedition, I announced my desire to find out what had caused the pirates to flee. "What exactly do you want to see?" Pacheco asked. I didn't know what to answer, so the question just hung in the air. Nevertheless, Asher and I boarded the little inflatable and headed out.

Once we arrived at the place where the "pirate" boats had been, we got into the water and dove to the bottom.

It took a long time for what we found to sink into our minds and truly register. Perhaps it was the gray color of the sharks' backs, that gift of evolution which camouflages them as they rise from the dark bottoms in pursuit of their unwitting prey, that initially hid from my eyes the drama of what had occurred. But then I felt the "bite."

In the movies, music prepares us for what's about to happen. Drama takes longer to build up in the silence that surrounded us. Realization crept in slowly, like a cold current crawling underneath my diving suit and slithering up my spine, until I saw in my mind the events that had led up to the scene we now witnessed. I caught Asher's eyes as he turned his head towards me. It's nearly impossible to surprise Asher (the former commando who has already seen everything), but this did. His eyes were wide open, artificially enlarged behind the diving mask.

I psychologically distanced myself and shot the photos without allowing myself to feel, motivated by the admiration I have for sharks. The power of their menace in life is not diminished in death. I shot picture after picture of the inanimate pile, capturing frozen images of these giant creatures, fins cut off, thrown overboard to drown. I just kept shooting.

THE START
OF A QUEST

"IT'S NOTHING BUT DEAD SHARKS."

One by one, finless sharks were piled onto the pier. From a
fishing boat moored nearby in the port town of Puntarenas,
Costa Rica, two men unloaded the creatures in a smooth
rhythm, pulling them from the boat using an iron hook stuck in
the sharks' mouths, then hurling them overboard to the pier.
My hand automatically reached into the camera bag hung
around my neck. I was alone, not far from the divers' yacht I
had left at the end of my journey to Cocos Island. I pulled out
the camera and prepared to shoot. This would be the perfect
photographic follow-up to the graveyard of finned sharks I had
discovered gently undulating on the bottom of the ocean.

The pile before me, here on the gray pier, seemed less out of
place and less shocking, bereft of the exotic blend of horror and
attraction I had experienced underwater. Apparently, however,
I was out of place now, blocked from taking a photograph by
a short, heavyset, unshaved man who stood in front of me and
held a manual stop sign to my face.

A dragger heading out for a long trip about ten miles off the coast of Sihanoukville, Cambodia.
(opposite)

A hammerhead shark caught on a longline in Cocos Island, Costa Rica (pages 160–161)

Cochin, India One by one, sharks were piled onto a gray pier. This happens all around the world.

"No!" he said in a Spanish accent.

"Why?" I asked.

"Because *prohibido*."

I made a little show of looking for a sign along the pier. "Where does it say?"

"Captain don't allow."

"May I speak to him?"

"You speak." He smiled.

I heard laughter. People quickly gathered around us. Alone and a foreigner, I was easy prey for jokes. The captain said something in Spanish, and someone volunteered a translation: "You want to buy?"

But the captain did not need his help. "If you want—then buy." He pointed at the pile.

"No, thank you," I said. Then I uttered the automatic response familiar to every Western tourist: "I don't need any."

"Then buy the boat."

Now this was a surprise. I laughed. "I don't need a boat."

The interpreter volunteered again: "The captain also don't need the boat, but it belongs to him." They laughed.

"Thank you," I repeated. "I don't need a boat." But then it occurred to me, "Only to get on the boat and take pictures."

The captain understood something else, so my idea was upgraded: "Buy the boat and do what you want." He smiled.

Without realizing it, I was already bargaining. "How much do you want for taking pictures on the boat?" I asked him.

"Ten thousand—dollars!"

Now I laughed, disingenuously. "It's nothing but dead sharks," I said, playing my role in the negotiation.

But he kept playing his. "You can get what you want—dead sharks, live sharks. You can do what you want—bring sharks, take their pictures, eat them, sell them—whatever you want." He pointed to the two men who had stopped working because of the show, and suggested something that made them smile, as the others laughed.

Suddenly, the idea came to me: I could rent the boat, as is, with its crew, and shoot a shark-fishing expedition from beginning to end. I sensed something else starting to form within me as well, but couldn't quite put my finger on it.

Back at work, the two men threw another shark onto the pile. After a month of shooting underwater, my personal ocean "quota" was full—I'd had enough of the experience for now and was eager to return home. I told the captain I was leaving but would be back, and then we would talk. I introduced myself and he shook my hand as he offered his own name: Captain Carrera. In an act of benevolence or temptation, he gestured towards the pile of dead sharks and invited me to take a picture.

But I already had greater designs in mind.

WHERE IS THE TRUE NUMBER HIDING?

As had happened already so many times in the past, my photos led me to research, and the research, in turn, whetted my hunger for more photos. To be honest, information about shark hunting had already been stored somewhere deep in my consciousness, but I kept repressing it because of my respect and admiration for these creatures—the living ones, that is. So I never pursued it. Now, as I obsessively looked at the final photos of the finned sharks on the bottom of the ocean, the interest resurfaced, this time looming too large to ignore.

Naturally, it is hard to estimate the number of sharks swimming in the world's oceans; after all, we are not even really sure how many shark species exist. But when it comes

Fins spread out to dry under the sun in the fishing village of Thoothoor, Tamil Nadu, India.

to knowing how many sharks we kill, our inability to obtain even vague estimates is mindboggling. Current guesses are between 40 million and 100 million sharks hunted every year. Where is the true number hiding—on the piers, or on the bottom of the ocean? Perhaps the key to the mystery lies in the carefully packaged and coveted crates of shark fins, tombstones of once-mighty carnivores thrown thoughtlessly overboard.

I returned to Captain Carrera after several months. "We don't throw the sharks to the ocean after we cut their fins," he said with a sardonic smile, as if alluding to the mystery of the missing numbers. He added as an afterthought, "Only when there's no more room on the boat." Fins are money. Prodded by shark-fin traders, who often bribe them with equipment and goods, local fishers cater to the lucrative fin-soup market. In Hong Kong, for example, a bowl of the finest fin soup can cost $120. On the wholesale market, wet shark fins can command $100 per pound; dried fins cost double. Shark meat itself garners mere pennies per pound. It's no wonder the bodies are so readily discarded.

Ahead of this return trip to Costa Rica, I had told Asher that our journey was going to have a journalistic angle: I wanted to document the shark hunt and try to understand why it is so difficult to estimate how rampant shark hunting is. Asher didn't buy it for a second: "There's nothing there for you except more action—an adrenaline rush."

Captain Carrera held all of the bargaining power, given the fact that I came back for both his boat and his services as captain—nobody else would sail with me and my camera looking over his shoulder. The amount he asked also included "all the sharks we won't hunt, because of you." That's how he put it, and I didn't know whether to take credit for saving at least these few, or take debit for the sharks killed especially for the camera. Either way, I ended up buying both the boat's time and this inherent contradiction.

We boarded the 50-foot (15-meter) boat named *Morgan,* a name perhaps pulled from a yacht catalog. Captain Carrera led Asher and me to the interior, and pointed to ice blocks (for cooling the meat) waiting there with eerie promise. The whiff of cold air made me suddenly afraid. Once more I felt out of depth, on the brink of venturing into uncharted territory governed by alien rules. As I always do in those moments, I looked at my camera bag and summoned a trait inherent in all photographers to protect me from disaster. Call it emotional imperviousness, insensitivity, you name it—it has protected me so far, perhaps even preselecting me for this profession, and I had to trust it. Nothing can hurt me when I am behind the steel door of my camera, looking at the world through a viewfinder. And, of course, I also had Asher.

CASTING FOR ANSWERS

When Time Seemed to Stand Still

We headed out to sea. It was a three-day voyage to Cocos Island. I knew the way there, and I knew that the sharks awaited us. Asher quickly went to sleep below deck. I stood outside, leaning on the railing and looking out to the horizon. The crew moved constantly about in a sort of active frenzy, making it impossible to differentiate individuals among the ubiquitous sailors. Only after we had made some headway did the traffic on deck subside. When the men lay down to rest, I could begin see their individual faces. They smiled at me. But just as the picture became clear, the sea started rising, and I found myself throwing up in their presence. I tried to overcome the sickness, just as I had fought to overcome trembling limbs in the faraway freezing waters of New England. The sailors chatted—they had no interest in me or my weak stomach. The motor churned, the boat rose and fell, and time seemed to stand still.

The meals brought up to the deck in metal containers didn't help pass the time—they were all alike: rice with something or something with rice for breakfast, lunch, and dinner. There was also very strong coffee made by filtering it through a sock again and again. After the first week of sailing and fishing they would run out of fresh coffee and switch to Nescafé. "Coffee—and, of course, the cigarettes that go with it—is the one thing you do not want to run out of," said Carrera, "because your crew gets very upset. And no one wants an upset crew." Luckily, they never ran out of Nescafé.

Below deck, there were double-decker metal frames for bunk beds, but the men preferred to spread their mattresses out in the open air and sleep with rough woolen blankets wrapped around them. When the sun came up in the morning, they would just pull the blankets up over their heads and continue to sleep off the previous hard day's tough physical labor. At first, I wondered why they opted to sleep on deck, but after two days of sailing I understood the reason they didn't go to the bunks below.

You can get rid of many things when you're at sea, but you can't get rid of the smell. Fishing boats are impregnated with memories in the form of smell. No matter what you do, the odors remain long after you scrub the boat with every possible detergent. The stench attaches itself to every surface and material, be it wood, metal, or cloth. I'd bet that even the rats in the boat's belly and the albatrosses in the skies above are affected by it. Diesel engine smoke, which often makes me nearly faint, cannot overpower the smell on deck. Below deck, the stench is simply unbearable.

Captain Carrera, *left,* **and crew.** Over repetitive 24-hour baiting, the boat will haul 50 to 150 sharks.

It Came for Blood

When we finally arrived off the shores of Cocos, the crew members began lowering the longline into the water, dropping it to a depth of 33 to 82 feet (10 to 25 meters). The hooks were spaced about 33 feet apart along the line and were baited with squid, tuna, mackerel, or any other fish with an intense scent that attracts sharks.

As the baited hooks made their way into the water, a flight of albatrosses tried to catch a meal. "We must do something about those birds," Carrera said, and cursed in his native tongue. "They feast on our fish but sometimes also die on the hook." Nobody wants an albatross on the hook, not just because it is an unintended loss of life, but because the bird represents the lost soul of a fisherman drowned at sea—a drowning albatross with a hook stuck in its throat is blatant bad luck.

I was eager for the sharks to arrive—hammerheads, threshers, blacktips, whitetips, silvertips, silkies, or Galapagos—all known to me from past excursions in these waters. Captain Carrera eagerly anticipated the sharks, too—or at least the sharks' fins.

Fishing, like photography, is all about waiting. I am used to waiting for good shots of sharks, but I had never photographed, nor ever seen—even in a picture—a shark hanging on a hook underwater. A gnawing doubt set in: Did I really want to see this?

The ocean was rising. I stood on the deck, trying to obey the cliché rule of focusing on the horizon lest I lose my lunch again. Every now and then a wave would crash over the deck and drench me, but going down to the putrid cabin below was unthinkable. As the deck danced below my feet, I held on to whatever I could to help keep me steady—first the railing, then the wheelhouse, then the bow rope. Meanwhile, the fishermen kept rolling out the longline. When the line stopped, the boat stopped, as if anchored in place by the power of hooks.

In the morning, we started to haul. The four men on the deck passed what seemed like a wave of air from hand to hand in harmonious pantomime movements. Only a sunray peeping through the clouds betrayed, in a momentary glimpse, the nylon thread stretching from their hands to the water. At first, only empty hooks piled up on deck. And then I saw it creeping to starboard—the first shark. In my mind, I completed the picture of gracious tail movements underwater. The shark started batting its tail wildly, its jaws opening and shutting in wild jolts. The indomitable crewmen flexed their muscles as a counterweight to the victim's twitching that added force to its solid mass.

I asked the captain to stop the haul and leave the shark in the water. Asher and I dove in under the boat. I approached the shark.

I have had many close encounters with sharks—sharks circling around me, sharks approaching me threateningly, sharks brushing and clashing against me. I have even had a shark bite my hand through a chain mail suit. But I had never until that moment seen a shark fighting for its life. As luck would have it, just like the first shark I ever

The baited longline before being lowered into the water.

encountered, this, too, was a hammerhead. It went limp after a final spasm, but even so, I looked for signs of life in the body now swaying helpless in the waves. With trepidation, I reached out and touched it. A dead shark is still a shark, and I was afraid that the hook stuck in its mouth would somehow tear loose, reanimating the beast and all its might.

Now I had to stabilize my body and take the shot. I motioned toward Asher and began shifting my position so that the shark would be between us. It was not easy to maneuver

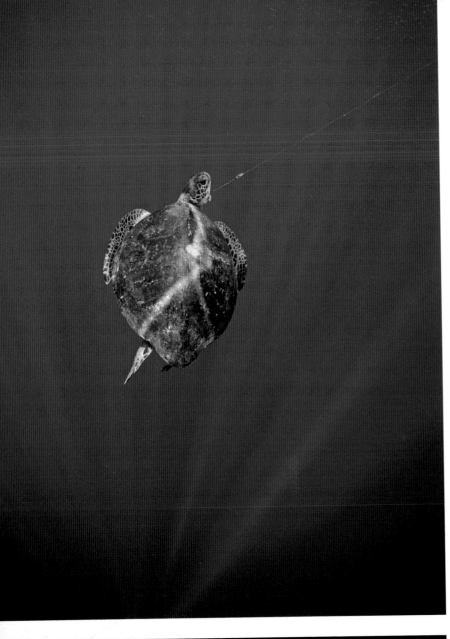

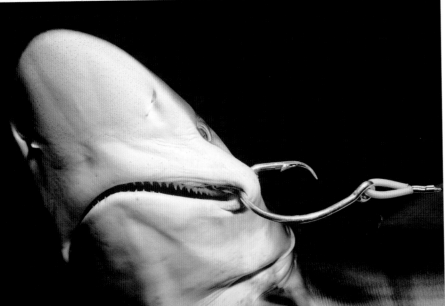

because the currents were strong and the waves were high. But I had all the time in the world—*this* shark would wait for me. To my surprise, for the first time in all of our years underwater, Asher showed signs of impatience. He had never rushed me before, even when floating aimlessly beside me in the water, fighting cold and boredom. I ignored him and took the pictures. Then I rose above water and motioned to the captain to keep pulling the thread until the next one showed up. I thought I could spend the entire dive that way, in one position as an assembly line of sharks paraded by. However, the next shark changed my plans. It wasn't on a hook, but was very much alive and hungry. Just like me, it came for blood. I now realized why Asher was anxious—sharks on the line meant sharks in the water. We carefully withdrew, went back to the boat, and stayed there.

On that day alone, a thousand hooks hung in different depths underwater were brought up to the boat along with a bountiful catch of yellowfin tuna, dorado, swordfish, marlin, one manta ray, and a few turtles.

Of course, the main attraction was the sharks: scalloped hammerheads, blacktips, and bigeye threshers, each anywhere from under three to fully ten feet long.

Armed with machetes, the crew sliced off their fins.

Two men with hooked poles about three feet (one meter) long dragged the finned sharks—some still alive—to the side of the boat and over the gunwale. The clear water swallowed the corpses one after another. Apparently, there was no room for them today, even though the storage rooms were still empty.

I looked at Asher. He read my mind and shook his head assertively, knowing what I was up to. But I rose and he followed me, his entire body protesting. We dove down, and then looked up. A few minutes later, I had what I had come for.

Turtles were among the bycatch. I freed some of them, but many were already dead. (top left and opposite)

A juvenile shark among the catch—evidence of how the sharks' population is being fished out faster than they can reproduce. (bottom left)

I don't recall ever getting out of the water with air left in my tanks and my camera still loaded, and feeling satisfied. But that one shot was enough for me. I gestured to Asher, not with the conventional gesture for "Let's go up," but with a gesture that meant something like, "Enough is enough."

Keeping only the sharks' fins and discarding the bodies increases a boat's capacity by 2,000 percent. Every boat that fins harvests the equivalent catch of twenty boats. **The still-living shark** is thrown overboard to drown in its own waters.

We went up on deck again, and I asked the captain to head back to port after they finished hauling all the fish. Carrera nodded in agreement. By noontime we started sailing. I saw the crewmen untying the knots that had formed in the longline. Routine in the aftermath.

Late in the afternoon, the crew started throwing the baited longline back into the water again. I looked at Carrera in askance and he gestured "one" with an upright finger. I could interpret it any way I liked—he could have meant one more round or one more shark. I wanted to protest, but I had no case. Back on land, I had asked the captain that the crew members ignore our presence and do their thing. And so they did.

Crossing the Longline

Come evening, the crewmen rested a bit. Two of them approached me and looked at the camera. They wanted me to take their pictures with the bloody knives and clothes. I acquiesced like an automaton. Somebody brought me terrible coffee, but its warmth melted me. I snapped portraits of the men. They didn't care if they would ever see the pictures, they just wanted me to have a souvenir so that I'd remember them from the other end of the world. Some of the crew pulled out their cell phones and asked to take my picture. Someone started washing the blood off the deck. I was struck by the innocence of the act: This was the nature of things. A fish is a fish. Who can say whether the suffering of a creature "drowning" in air after being raised in a net, cramped between hundreds of his own and other species, is better or worse than the suffering of a shark literally drowning in water with its fins cut off?

Carrera came out of the wheelhouse and sat down next to me, a cigarette hanging from his lip. I tried to start a conversation, and pointed to the storage rooms below. "Tuna? Swordfish? Marlin? Shark?" I listed the majestic species, the kings of this ocean.

Carrera just nodded. "You have cigarettes?" he asked.

I fished out a pack.

Some recent estimates claim that humans are fishing out sharks at twice their capacity to reproduce. The United Nations Food and Agriculture Organization estimates that over the last fifty years, the worldwide catch of elasmobranches (the group that includes sharks, skates, and rays) has escalated from 200,000 to 800,000 metric tons a year. Some observers consider this to be a conservative figure, particularly because bycatch numbers (accidental catch) are not included.

Every three to five years, humans kill as many sharks as there are people in the United States, according to Dr. Samuel Gruber, professor of marine biology at the University of Miami's Rosenstiel School of Marine and Atmospheric Science.

Asher Gal shark hunting off Cocos Island approaches a black marlin on a longline.

"Marlboro, Kent, Winston, Virginia," he said. He took the pack, lit a new cigarette with the one in his mouth and placed a third behind his ear. I offered the rest to the men, and they followed suit.

"How many sharks do you throw to the water every time?" I asked. "Isn't it better to sell them?"

Carrera got the hint. "How many? What—are you the police?" He laughed. "Maybe a scientist? They always ask, 'How many this? How many this and this?' We can help scientists—we can take all the sharks out of the sea so they can count." Then he asked, smiling, "You have no dead sharks back home in America?"

I had never thought about it. I shrugged. It was as though "hunted shark" had become a species in its own right.

"So what do you have there, in your sea in America?" he asked.

With Bostonian pride, I answered, "Cod. A lot of it." But upon uttering the fish's name, cod, I remembered that this was no longer true. The factories producing our native Gloucester dish—fish sticks—import their cod from Alaska. Regardless, the captain didn't know that name. I tried another one: "flounder." When he shrugged, I pantomimed the fish, tilting my head to a horizontal posture, leaning it on one hand, and using the other to move the lower eye and stick it to my upper cheek. Carrera laughed and said the name in his native tongue, although I am quite sure he never saw it in his native waters.

The water was calm. The sun was setting. Someone served another round of coffee. I thought about the photographs I had taken. The fishermen weren't the only ones who had had a good catch that day. Then it struck me that this boat was not merely a means of taking me from one point to the other. Rather, the swaying boat itself, neither land nor water, was my destination. Nobody said a word and I told myself that this silence was a fisherman language. I was happy with my catch, but I felt as if I had crossed a line—the longline, if you will.

HOW CAN YOU CAPTURE SOMETHING THAT IS MISSING?

Photographs of live sharks lay spread on the light table in my studio. I had been invited to give a lecture to a Boston diving club and these images would form the climax of my presentation. Directly beside the light table lay the slides from my last trip to Cocos Island—the shark-hunting trip. I hadn't yet filed them away because I didn't know where they should go. They didn't belong to any of the established categories in my photo library. So they had just been lying there in boxes since they were developed.

Then an idea came to me. I guess it was my usual urge to break routines that led me to realize that I should insert some of the graphic images of the hunted sharks into my regular lecture about the beauty of the underwater world. They would inject a "flow of new blood" into my talk in more ways than one.

Scalloped hammerhead sharks, Cocos Island, Costa Rica

179

A new focus, fish in "open" air. A gill net laid by Bedouin fishermen on a coral reef produces butterfly fish, parrotfish, and one picasso triggerfish. Only the parrotfish will be eaten, the rest will be thrown back to the sea to die, if not dead already.

I never had a chance to give that particular, original talk because the lecture got cancelled. But the juxtaposition of these two completely different storylines—the majesty of the living ocean, and the brutality of shark hunting—stuck with me.

It became a fixture of my thoughts, even of my conversations. I'd ask my unsuspecting friends, "How many people do you think are attacked by sharks every year around the world?" Most got close to the right answer, guessing between 50 and 100. (There were 72 attacks on humans including 10 deaths in 2013.) But then I'd ask, "How many sharks do you think are killed by humans every year around the world?" They weren't close this time, usually guessing in the thousands or tens of thousands. The right answer? Between 80 and 100 *million*. The answer shocked my friends. One said, "If that's right, then sooner or later they will all be gone."

Through these conversations, something from deep in my mind gained clarity and focus. As a photographer, I always concentrate on what is in front of me—that's my job. I have a romantic (and banal) notion of myself as a hunter—I track, follow, ambush, and capture prey, and my success feeds my family. Like a hunter, I don't waste time thinking about what isn't there. If prey eludes me, it is likely a lack of luck or a lack of skill. But what if the reason wasn't that simple?

It used to be that I would never come up from a dive without having seen at least one manta, maybe a hammerhead or two (but more probably three or four). I always saw numerous whitetip reef sharks and a few blacktips, too. Every once in a while, I'd see sharks that made unpredictable but frequent appearances, such as the whale shark, tiger shark, oceanic whitetip, and mako. The sightings beat out the pulse of the ocean that surrounded me from all directions, reverberating in my heart. But as I thought about it, I realized that this pulse had been getting weaker and weaker. Where had all the big fish gone? The heroes of my "professional childhood" were disappearing. I had never stopped to think about the reasons, and had never—until my trip to Cocos—stopped to think about the people who fished out these creatures from the water.

They had been right there, in the background, for years: Fishermen of all kinds had lurked at the edge of my vision, but never in focus. If anything, their presence had always been a bit of a disturbance. After all, we were in competition, battling for the same hunting grounds. On my dives, I could often see traces of their crude craft—bits of rope, forgotten nets, and broken corals. But now I realized that I had also been able to *feel* their presence in the thinning populations of my personal passion—the living creatures I capture in photographs.

It is difficult to pinpoint the exact moment when my new quest crystallized, but I can say that somehow, out of the dissonance cast between those two groups of images on my light table, my fishing journey around the world was born.

I was going to turn my camera in a different direction to tell a different story.

PART III

THE LAST HUNTING GROUNDS

NETS COMBING THE SEA— TRAWLING

SCRAPING THE BOTTOM: NEW ENGLAND

I had started my photography career in New England, evolving a toughness that has seen me through countless dangerous and treacherous dives. In the light of my new mission, I thought about the New England fishermen who had been the heroes of a glorious past, and who were now subjects of the troubled present. I decided to start there.

First, I had to find a fisherman.

Massachusetts Bay is sharply divided between Cape Cod to the south and Cape Ann to the north. Gloucester, which lies on Cape Ann, is a beacon in the history of American fishing. The fishermen of Gloucester are a prideful bunch and consider themselves to be *true* blue-collar fishermen, in part because they use draggers instead of hooks and lines. I made the town of Gloucester my home base again, this time for fishing instead of diving.

The *Padre Pio*'s catch from the deep and followers in the sky. (opposite)
Jangada, a wooden raft used by Brazilian fishermen. (pages 182–83)

I looked for a fisherman who would be willing to let me join him on expeditions. No one would take me. I felt as if I were trying to catch a fish in an unfamiliar sea, casting out only a net of suspicion. So I invited myself to a meeting of Gloucester fishermen. To fish in these waters, I'd have to use enticing bait. Employing a slightly exaggerated Bostonian accent, I showed them what I had to offer—photographs of fish taken in "our New England ocean."

When a fisherman named Joe Orlando saw my photograph of a goosefish, he got very excited. "I have never seen them there—*in* the water. What a beautiful fish!" Joe knew what it took to get those photographs in his rough ocean. In this way, Joe and I chose each other.

I joined Joe, his son Mario, and his friend Franco aboard his trawler, the *Padre Pio*. Together, on and off for more than two decades, we sailed over the troughs of the past and the crests of the present in search of our fish tale.

I think that if Joe were to tell his story, he would start from the end, so I will, too. One late afternoon he called me. "*Padre Pio*," which represented his livelihood—his means of feeding not only himself, but his father and his son, too—and even took his grandchildren over the horizon of Gloucester Harbor, "was sold." He couldn't bring himself to say, "I sold it." What he did say was, "I can't do this anymore. I can't fish."

A Bridge of Fish

Joe moved to Massachusetts from Sicily at age five, but the roots of his story go back centuries. The bridge uniting Gloucester and Europe across the ocean is represented by the old saying, "You could walk from Europe to America on the backs of cod." Cod was the main attraction for fishermen of both continents. For the past 400 years, American fishermen have been mining the dangerous waters from the Grand Banks in Canada down to the Gulf of Maine, Georges Bank off Cape Cod, and the inshore grounds of Stellwagen Bank and Jeffrey's Ledge. This area has long supplied fish to the tables of the world.

The fishermen's harvesting methods, however, have changed. The old salt banker schooners, upon which the fish were preserved in salt imported from Sicily until ice became readily available, gave way to technological breakthroughs that hurled motorized boats through the waters, transforming the very nature of fishing in the process. Then came the trawlers, which combed the bottom of the ocean, indiscriminately catching whatever could be found there.

Over the years, trawler fishermen have followed demand and emptied the waters of one species after another: first cod, then haddock, then redfish. Success was quick and bitter. It didn't take long for people to realize that the ocean's bounty is far from boundless, and that such indiscriminate mining disrupts ecological balances and irreversibly depletes ocean resources. Scientists and ocean-lovers warned against the drastic depletion of fish populations and tried several methods of regulation to help temper the

damage, including increasing net mesh sizes, closing entire areas to fishing, and imposing fishing quotas. But for a long time, these recommendations were not enforced and the waters remained wide open to fishermen from all over the world.

Only in the late 1970s (after the Magnuson Fishery Conservation and Management Act of 1976) were the territorial waters of the United States clearly demarcated and made forbidden to foreign fishermen. This, accompanied by technological advances that significantly increased catch volumes, led to a brief period of prosperity in the Northeast.

During the 1980s boom, Joe bought his own boat and christened it *Padre Pio* after his father's boat. Sweet as it was, though, this boom was quickly cut short; the fisheries collapsed.

Mario Orlando holding a cod—every fisherman in Gloucester probably has a picture like this.

IT AIN'T A TOURIST YACHT

This photograph was taken on a stormy night in February. The boat rocked in rhythm with two terrible storms—one raging outside and one raging in my mind. All that terrible night, I clung to the pole of my bunk bed, my refuge from the wave-swept deck above. Staying below, my head emerging from under my blanket only to make use of the barf bag, I could picture the 20-foot walls of water repeatedly rising against the bow and breaking across the boat.

Finally, morning came, or so I guessed—it was still dark deep inside the *Padre Pio*, but I heard the squeaking loudspeaker coughing out voices that I imagined were prayers. In the middle of the storm, even I became a believer. I went out on deck as first light broke. It was a relief to see a horizon again; even though it was still jumping erratically up and down in the continuing storm, I managed to keep my bearings.

"A fishing boat," Joe said to me as I approached on unsteady legs, "is built to do just that. It ain't any wave-ironing tourist yacht." I felt he enjoyed tormenting me a bit. The rest of the crew had all crowded into the wheelhouse. Oddly enough, the higher the waves, the more peaceful their movements were. They were safe havens unto themselves, each anchored on two steady legs stretching down to the bottom of the ocean. Surprisingly, my sickness started to fade away; perhaps I drew comfort from their proximity.

Joe was navigating the *Padre Pio* 160 miles (about 260 kilometers) off the Gloucester coast on the rich grounds of Georges Bank. In spite of the big storm he decided to stay in the water. Storms are very good for prices—the fewer fishermen who dare to venture out, the smaller the supply available to meet the constant demand. But a 20-foot sea makes it impossible to drag a trawl along the bottom. We spent forty-eight endless hours in the same spot, waiting to start fishing. I could not do anything to change this decision; I was a guest (vomiting) on this boat. While I worried about the conditions, knowing how far away we were from any safe port, I was sure these fishermen never gave them a thought.

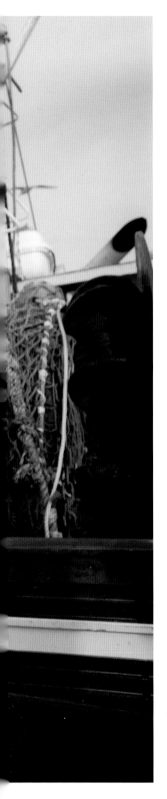

The *Padre Pio* became my fishing base, just as the waters of New England represented my diving base from which I ventured to dive around the world. For more than twenty years, my fishing trips off Gloucester were like visits back in time to my childhood landscapes. I had longed for these experiences from the distance of time and place, but now, realizing the sad change in this fishery, I often just as powerfully wished my present experiences would end so that I could distance myself again.

When he was a child, Joe accompanied his father on the original *Padre Pio*. It wasn't long before he became the youngest captain in the Gloucester fishing fleet. Joe has been a master of these waters for over thirty years, but he never relied solely on his past experiences or the huge database he carries in his head. Joe had state-of-the-art instruments on his deck—two of each kind, just to be safe. He had GPS, radar, and both a magnetic and a satellite compass. His top-of-the-line sonar fish-finders allowed him to see both the sea bottom and the water column. He had CB radio for boat-to-boat communication and VHF radio with a much longer range that he used to listen to the radio chatter of the thirty inshore draggers in the area. Every now and then, Joe would pick up his binoculars and try to see what their nets had brought up.

Some of the captains chattered nonstop in Sicilian dialect, peppered with colorful English words and expressions. When I asked Joe what they were saying, he replied that they were reporting very poor tows "no matter what." After a pause, he added—smiling, "Remember, Jeff, all fishermen are liars."

Joe knows the true numbers. For years he carefully documented every scrap of fishing-related data and used it to direct his boat in the waters that had blessed him with bounty in the past. Sadly, his charts were like a doomed airliner's black box, recording data that documented failure and destruction.

Captain Joe Orlando and his state-of-the-art "eyes." (above)

A fisheries observer, *background left*, takes notes regarding the catch as Mario cleans codfish. (opposite)

True Fishermen's Lies

One January morning, I got a call from Joe telling me that a certain area (in fishing terms, a "quadrangle") was scheduled to reopen next week. This quadrangle had been closed for the past nine months as part of fishery management plan to help stem overfishing and rebuild depleted fish stocks. Joe said the entire fleet would be there and that the first few tows of the net should bring in big catches. The area would open at exactly one minute after midnight.

We left the dock at 9:30PM and I could see many other inshore draggers pushing off, too. Every boat wanted to be on location well ahead of time. Each captain had his favorite tow route and wanted to try his best to get it. When the *Padre Pio* put its net in the water, there would be very little guesswork involved. Joe had read the records and would place the net exactly where he wanted it, perhaps retracing the course he ran ten years earlier on this particular week in January and hoping for the same success.

As the clock struck twelve, Joe and Mario set out the net. The ocean floor was about 660 feet (200 meters) below, and they towed that bottom for two hours. All the while, Joe kept a careful eye on his electronics, especially his fish-finders. Years of tows had taught Joe the subtle indicators of when to bring up the net. Too early, and he would not have the good catch he needs; too late, and the net would be too full, with much of the catch in less than prime condition. Finally, Joe made the decision. He woke his son Mario from his catnap and gave the all-important command: "Let's haul back."

Both Mario and Joe wore comfortable sweat pants and shirts inside the cabin. The radiator kept things toasty warm. But outside was a different story. The winter temperature hovered around 20°F (−6°C), but the wind chill made it feel much colder. Much of the work outside was physical, which helped to keep them warm, but specialized clothing was still required. First, they pulled on oilskin pants that came all the way up to cover their chests. Next they stepped into steel-toed deck boots that protected their feet and kept them dry. Mario pulled on a New England Patriots hooded sweatshirt for good measure. They both zipped up oilskin coats and put waterproof gloves over cotton ones before stepping out onto the deck. It was like stepping onto a different planet. The wind was howling, causing the salt spray to slap our faces. The seagulls seemed to smile at what promised to be a five-star feast.

Powerful deck lights illuminated the boat and the surrounding choppy sea. Two powerful winches were turned on—the hauling back of the net began. Steel cables slowly and steadily pulled the net up from the ocean bottom. Within five minutes the "barn doors," thousand-pound rectangular steel slabs, made their appearance. These doors kept the net spread open as it dragged along the bottom. Once at the surface, they were unhooked and attached to the side of the boat. The net continued its trip toward us. Within a few minutes we saw the buoys that helped to hold open the cod end, which was the part of the trawl where fish were retained. One more minute and we would know what we had caught.

As the cod end was hauled up onto the boat I rejoiced at the sight of the net bulging to its limit with cod and yellowtail flounder. I could see lobster claws, occasional skates, and more than a few monkfish pressed tight against the net.

I also noticed that Joe and Mario showed absolutely no emotion at the sight of the full net. I guessed that hauling near-empty nets over the last years had given them a new perspective on this sporadic success. They were completely neutral, neither excited nor disappointed. I, on the other hand, was jubilant. Although over the years of fishing with them I had photographed their catches hundreds of times, it had never been the same twice. Seeing the fish faces pressed against the net, I am never sure where to aim my lens. This time, I once again became lost in the image and was reminded why I kept returning to the *Padre Pio*.

The bulging net was positioned in the middle of the deck. Joe worked the winch as Mario grabbed the rope that would release the catch onto the deck. Mario pulled on the rope, and a soft "whoosh" sounded as the net opened and a huge sampling of the richness that used to live on the bottom of the North Atlantic flowed out. An amazing mix of sea life flopped and squirmed on deck in a carpet of catch easily more than a foot deep. Joe and Mario did not waste time admiring their haul. Instead, they rushed to get the net back

An amazing assortment of sea life rises from the bottom of the North Atlantic to carpet the deck. (opposite, top and middle) After sorting, the bycatch is then returned to the ocean. (opposite, bottom)

Sorting, gutting, cleaning, packing on ice—fishing is a bloody, labor-intensive job. (above)

JOE'S SICILIAN HERITAGE

Part of my personal interest in fishing and Joe in particular can be traced back to an almost accidental acquaintance I made with the Sicilian bluefin tuna-fishing culture in a diving trip well before I met Joe.

"There's a photo-op for you," said my friend Marcello, a great Italian photographer. "A chance to shoot underwater. You will love this—you could swim among hundreds of huge tuna fish, maybe even sharks, seconds before they're slaughtered."

This is how I first learned about the *mattanza*. I admit that Sicily's mattanza fishing ritual attracted me back then because of its Hemingway-esque romanticism: men, hunting, spears, blood. But all that is left of this romanticism today is nostalgia for the days in which everyone believed there was no end to the oceans' bounty. When, years later, I mentioned my experience to Joe, naturally he knew about the tradition I described—it is part of his heritage. "The mattanza—this culture is disappearing," he said, "together with the bluefin tuna itself." "Mattanza" comes from the Spanish word *matar*, meaning "to kill." It's a term used by Italians to denote both Mafia massacres and an ancient ceremonial method of tuna fishing in which the fishermen spear the enormous silvery fish and use the power of their arms to pull the tuna from the blood-red sea.

Marcello wanted me to complement his above-water mattanza shots with never-before-seen underwater photos from within the "death chamber"—the place where the tuna fish are rounded up for slaughter, having been ensnared in the *tonnare*, a complex system of netted traps.

The event was to take place in Favignana, the principal Aegadian Island known as the "Queen of the Tonnare." This small island owes its name to the mistral, the ancient *favonius* ("favorable [strong] wind") that pushes the tuna into the traps. The mistral signals the arrival of the tuna caravan during their run towards the Mediterranean. This is the only time ocean tuna come together in shoals; they are normally solitary. The tuna move in a cubic formation that maximizes the chances for external fertilization of their eggs. When the caravan reaches the Mediterranean, having traveled up to 150 miles (240 kilometers) a day, the older *golfitani* join up with the shoal. Golfitani are tuna born in the Mediterranean, who after having reached sexual maturity at about age four will undertake their first run towards the Atlantic at the end of the reproductive period.

On the morning of the hunt, shortly before dawn, the white boat of the *rais* (Arabic for "boss") went to the site, accompanied by about a hundred fishermen aboard eight large black boats and

two 65-foot-long (20-meter) vessels that could each carry up to 75 tons of fish. At the rais's direction, the fishermen lowered approximately 10 miles (15 kilometers) of nets, forming an obligatory route for the tuna that would lead them to the *vaso*—the neck. The entire vaso of the tonnare is divided into a number of large chambers separated by vertical nets. The fishermen progressively narrow the chambers, forcing the tuna to pass from one chamber to the next until they are finally pushed into the death chamber.

The tuna arrived and entered the tonnare, speeding toward their fate as the fishermen followed the rais's commands. The fishermen cadenced their movements by singing the *cialoma*, a traditional working song of Sicilian fishermen led by the *cialomatore* with a voice reminiscent of an Arab muezzin. After a few minutes, many fish were already dead, killed by the lack of water or crushed by other members of the shoal. The chorus became more urgent as the nets filled. As the fishermen pulled up the heavy net with their hands,

the floor of the death chamber rose toward the surface. The fish went crazy. With no room to move or way to escape, they thrashed against each other and the sea turned red with their blood.

At this point, it is customary for a local diver to jump in to make sure there are no sharks among the tuna before the spearing begins. (Tuna fishermen call sharks *piscumalu*, or "evil fish.") This is when Marcello had arranged for me to enter the scene. Introducing me to the fishermen as a famous underwater diver and expert photographer, he had persuaded them, against their safety rules, to let me join the company diver in the tuna net to photograph.

I had rented double steel tanks like the ones used by the company diver. Double steel tanks are very heavy and I wasn't used to them. The company diver saw my weight belt and advised me to use much less weight, but having just flown over from my diving kingdom in the Red Sea, I was brimming with confidence and rejected the advice. I slid over the side of the boat and descended like a boulder about 130 feet (40 meters) to the ocean floor. I had to leave my weight belt behind to get up to the surface. Everyone had a good laugh at the expense of the "famous undersea photographer." I was told—in no uncertain terms—that I had experienced my first and last dive in the tuna nets—I was too great a risk.

Marcello, however, went to work, charming the fishermen and offering to buy many people extravagant dinners and copious amounts of alcohol. Finally, they agreed to give the foolish American one more chance.

WHAT MAKES ONE A CAPTAIN?

As I watched Mario at the wheel of the *Pio*, I thought he looked like a captain. I supposed he came by it honestly, trained from the very first moment his father, Joe, let him on board and ordered him to clean up the fish on deck. Both the profession and the status are hereditary. At the end of the day, sophisticated equipment on a fishing boat can make life much easier for a captain, but the difference between a captain and a "deck hand" is the difference between a quarterback and any other football player—the ability to make split-second decisions. As a defensive tackle, I had only mass and speed, and was always astonished to see how little time passed between the quarterback taking his hands out of their warmers and the quarterback getting flattened on the ground. But in those few seconds, the most important decisions of the game were made.

The ability to make decisions is still not enough to make a captain; something extra is needed for that special mix. I suppose everyone destined to become a captain hears about this special something in fish tales. For Joe and Mario (one day, perhaps, Mario will leave his fish stick factory and become a captain), the most famous Gloucester fish tale on the subject is the story of a legendary dory man named Howard Blackburn. One stormy night, Howard and his friend Tom Welch were

aboard a dory setting the trawl of their mother schooner when they lost their bearings in the fog and could not find their way back. They rowed through the whole night, desperately searching for their schooner, until Tom froze to death. Howard lost his gloves and soon enough his hands became frozen to the oars—but he kept rowing. For a hundred miles, Howard rowed the dory, and his dead dorymate, back to shore. He lost his fingers and his toes, but he survived.

Mario awakened me from reverie and told me that it was time to make dinner. He jumped downstairs to prepare pasta and scallops. He cut paper-thin slices of garlic with a razor blade and showed me how they liquefy when placed in a pan of hot olive oil. Then he added tomatoes and onions to make a sauce. Lecturing me to "never overcook seafood," he cooked the scallops for only a few minutes. Spaghetti was made; a salad was dressed with olive oil and vinegar, and a large loaf of Italian scali bread was placed on the table. The others joined us, and as dinner was served Mario announced: "No one eats better than the Sicilian fishermen of Gloucester."

What is it, then, that in addition to decision-making makes a captain a captain? I guess you could call it persistence—and pride.

Pictured above is Mario sorting a catch of skate, yellowtail flounder, codfish, goosefish on board the *Padre Pio* in a blustery snow storm in February.

in the water. Within fifteen minutes, it was back on the bottom, fishing. Joe put the boat on autopilot, checked his many electronic instruments, gave the engine room a quick look, and joined Mario on deck to help sort, gut, and clean the cod, wash the flounder, and pack the catch on ice in crates. This is a bloody, labor-intensive job. Mario made some cuts with his practiced movements. Before I knew it, gills and guts were torn free to lie on the deck floor. Hundreds of herring gulls circled in anticipation.

The bycatch—an assortment of sea stars, crabs, unwanted skates, a gigantic electric torpedo ray, and all the undersized lobsters and fish—were shoveled over the side, some still alive, some already dead. Now the herring gulls got their turn. Shovel after shovel of fish innards went overboard, and they went absolutely berserk. The noise was deafening as they fought over the spoils. They were gone within minutes, leaving us with the noise of the wind as it gusted across the deck, and of the sea as it slapped against the hull.

Drowning in Numbers

Every three or four trips, an official fisheries observer boards boats such as the *Padre Pio* to conduct statistical analyses: How many fish are caught in the net? How many species and how many specimens of each? How much of the catch is bycatch? How wide is the mesh? What is the size of the area trawled?

Numbers are also critical for the fishing captains: How big is the legal fishing area? How many days can they fish each year? What is the quota for each species? What is the legally permitted size of each? How big is the fine for violating any of these regulations? Finally, before casting their nets, they need to find out what other fishermen have hauled today, and what price their catch can fetch in the auction.

Everyone—scientists, fishermen, politicians, and environmentalists—are united in their love for the ocean and its creatures, and each party tries to understand the others' positions. But this is war: a war of numbers. Numbers are the weapons, but they often prove slippery, as difficult to hold onto as a fish in the water. And as in every war, every side has a point to make and defend. Justice, sometimes, is a matter of time and place. The fishermen claim that the scientists are documenting declines because they don't know where and when to search; the scientists claim that the fishermen fail to see the big picture, focusing only on their narrow firsthand observations. But what is the big picture and how can it be constructed? Scientists, say the fishermen, are just like military historians: Learn the lesson and prepare the army for . . . the previous war.

"Scientists are always one step behind," says Joe. "I'll give you a perfect example" (another fish tale). "One week, we had bad weather out at Stellwagen Bank at a time and place scientists had claimed there would be no cod. No one went out for four days. All of a sudden, it cleared up and we had good weather. I arrived to Stellwagen first, well ahead of everyone else. I did a twenty-minute tow and the fish-finders were all lit up. We had to haul

back. The cod end of the net came out like a balloon because the fish bellies expanded with air. I had to tie off six times and brought in six full cod ends—that's 12,000 pounds of just cod. When I got into the harbor I got another fisherman to help Mario and me clean the fish. It took us twelve hours—we were up to our waists in cod. The next day at auction I got $3.80 a pound for market cod and $4.40 a pound for large cod. We made $38,862 in that one twenty-minute tow."

In the 2004 regional fishery management plans to prevent overfishing (known as Amendment 13), scientists predicted and promised that the northern Atlantic fish populations would recover in ten years. Certain areas of New England waters were closed to fishing, quotas of various species were set, and a series of other regulations and guidelines came into effect. Fishermen were, and still are, very careful to observe these rules; they know that their future depends on the success of the stock. And if that weren't enough incentive, strictly enforced fines discourage violations.

In 2014, however, the scientists revised their optimistic assessments. They explained that their methodology may have been erroneous and that some factors are inherently difficult to account for, such as rising water ocean

A foot deep of richness: cod, yellowtail flounder, lobster, skates, dogfish sharks, monkfish, sea stars, crabs, electric torpedo rays, and more. (left)

"Illegal" size means a second chance for some fish. As for the others—a nice chance for the herring gulls. (above)

LOBSTER FISHING IN NEW ENGLAND—A SUCCESS STORY?

In December of 1990, I went to Monhegan Island off the coast of Maine to photograph the events of January 1: Trap Day, when the lobstermen of Monhegan Island put their traps in the water. The traps would be active for the next six months. Most lobstering is done from May through November along the coastal waters of Maine, but Monhegan lobstermen have always done things their way. They get a better price in the winter because there are fewer lobsters being caught. And Monhegan has the reputation of being very rich lobster grounds.

Although Trap Day has since been changed to October 1 to extend the season, the ritual remains the same. On this day, all of the island's thirteen lobster boats head out at the same time and claim their spots. Three days later, they pull in the traps and harvest their first catch. They will pull their traps every three days. If bad weather is forecasted, they might make an extra trip, pulling them right before the weather hits and making sure all their buoys are secure. Every buoy has three to four traps attached to it, placed at different depths depending on the bottom. It could be as shallow as 30 feet or as deep as 130 feet (9–40 meters).

Lobster has always been a very successful fishery, helped by strong conservation laws that are strictly enforced. For example, there are both minimum and maximum size limits. It usually takes a lobster six to seven years to reach legal size and sexual maturity. So all lobsters have a chance to reproduce before being caught. Also, if a female is carrying eggs on the underside of her tail she must be returned to the water.

Many fishery scientists feel that the decline in codfish has greatly helped the lobster industry. Codfish feed on the juvenile lobsters and this lack of predation has helped promote a lobster population explosion over the last decades.

temperatures and the water's changing chemical composition due to global warming. The bottom line was: There are still not enough fish. But by the time fish populations finally recover, there may be nobody left to catch them.

A Personal Perspective on the Changing Tides of North Atlantic Fishing

In 1976, at the age of twenty-four, Joe Orlando became the youngest skipper in the Gloucester fleet, directing a crew of six.

"Back in those days a one-day trip dragging the inshore waters would net 7,000 to 8,000 pounds of cod, 10,000 to 20,000 pounds of shrimp and 3,000 to 4,000 pounds of redfish," Joe says. "Fuel was cheap—and ice, insurance, gear, maintenance—what have you."

Here are several more changes Joe has witnessed since becoming a captain:

- The annual cod quota was reduced from 100,000 to 35,000 and finally to just 5,000 pounds.

- Yellowtail and winter flounder quotas have been reduced by over 60 percent.

- Monkfish can now be fished only 39 days a year.

- According to the National Oceanic and Atmospheric Administration (NOAA), the number of New England fishing boats fell from 1,019 in 2004 to just 344 today.

Countdown to Joe

When I started sailing on the *Padre Pio* with Joe, there were two other men on board: his son Mario and his friend Franco. The hauls kept dropping, and so did the quotas, and there was simply not enough to feed all three.

Franco left first.

Two remained: Joe and Mario.

The hauls kept dropping.

Mario left; he now works in a fish-stick factory. Like over 90 percent of the seafood in the United States, the fish are imported.

Joe was alone. What could a lone fisherman do with a 65-foot-long boat weighing 88 tons, powered by a 12-cylinder, 340-horsepower General Motors engine?

Joe sold the boat.

Perhaps he will buy himself a smaller boat one day and occasionally brave the seas and venture out alone to continue the tradition of his forefathers, save his honor, and breathe the winds of freedom blowing in from Gloucester's horizons. Perhaps he could, at least, reuse the name *Padre Pio*.

A VERY "RICH" BYCATCH: MOROCCO

Fighting the Elements

I had to go through seven kinds of hell in order to obtain a permit to board a fishing boat on Morocco's Atlantic coast. For the first time in all my fishing trips, I needed someone to sail the treacherous waters of bureaucracy before I could even set foot on deck. "There's a good reason for all the red tape," said Othman, my middleman, a vigorous journalist from Casablanca. "Fishing in Morocco is a serious business, a business managed by the state. It is one of the country's biggest employers. The government puts a lot of effort into modernizing fishing so as to maximize its export revenues."

Later, over an exquisite tagine of lamb with dates, Othman added, "As for the local market," he smiled, "the government tries to regulate our diets and to convince us—Moroccans!—to eat more fish." He took another bite of lamb. "Instead of meat."

Throughout our journey along the Atlantic coast, from Casablanca in the north to Agadir in the south, we helplessly dangled between local bureaucracy and the elements. Both seemed to be making a particular effort to prevent me from going out to sea. When the weather conditions were good and boats were going out to fish, I had to wait for an official permit to board one of them. By the time I would get it, the weather had changed and the boats withdrawn to shelter in the harbors and beaches. We tested our luck, going from one town to the next for two weeks; only when we reached Agadir, my last planned stop, did I finally get both a permit and a smiling sky.

Bad weather conditions force boats to withdraw to shelter on the beach in Morocco. (above)

Artisanal fishermen venturing out and returning with their catch. (opposite)

In terms of value, purse seiners bring in the most fish, but trawlers and longliners generate higher income because they catch the more prized species such as octopi. The majority of the fishing industry in Morocco consists of small-scale fisheries. Studies estimate that there are about 5,000 boats with 45,000 artisanal fishermen in Morocco, and it is generally assumed that the number of small fishing boats, such as canoes, is on the rise. These small wooden boats are less than 20 feet long, typically with outboard engines and a two- to four-member crew. They employ predominantly gill nets.

Artisanal fishermen follow their forefathers' traditions and often do not have any other employment options. The main challenge they face stems from their lack of education and consequent inability to adopt new techniques and methods. Another problem is that artisanal fishermen generally lack access to modern infrastructures like cold storage and transportation, which make it difficult to sell their goods in big city markets.

The Arabic text on the sign reads: القدس 3

AL QODS 3
8-936

The bycatch of a dragger turns a rich
ocean bottom into a Sahara.

On a Moroccan Dragger: Going After Octopus

My first night in the Atlantic waters off Agadir was on a dragger. We dragged our nets
about 20 miles (32 kilometers) from land. The mesh size was so small that almost nothing
could escape. What came up was an amazing variety of fish and invertebrate bottom
life. But the big money catch was octopus—the fishermen's main goal. Once the net
was emptied on deck, the octopi were first to get separated and collected in big burlap
bags. There was a huge amount of bycatch, much of it dead. Whatever gets caught at the
beginning of the dragging has little chance of surviving the crushing pressure in the net
over the three- to four-hour drag along the bottom. One can imagine how devastating this
method of fishing can be to the marine environment: a rich bottom, teeming with life,
turned into a Sahara by the trawlers.

On a Moroccan Purse Seiner: Going After a Big Small Fish

Coming back from the night fishing with the dragger, without a break, Othman and I got aboard a purse seiner to fish for sardines—small fish that loom very large in the Moroccan economy. We found a school of sardines and surrounded it with a net, using a smaller boat to help close the purse, and then hauled it in using heavy-duty winches.

There were about twenty-five fishermen on board, all engaged in the labor-intensive process of folding back the heavy net as it emerged. It was dark, and the wind started to blow strong. The seas were running high, and getting my footing was a real challenge. At one point, a gigantic wave broke over the bow and I—and my camera—got soaked. My motor-driven camera was completely destroyed. I might as well have thrown it right into the ocean. I have lost many cameras to waves over the years I've photographed fishing. There is not much one can do to prevent it besides encasing the cameras in plastic, but that makes them very difficult to work with.

The entire deck was soaked with seawater and rain. The net safely packed away, the cook brought out an enormous teakettle, and tiny glasses of scalding hot sweet tea were poured and passed around. We all had seconds. As we sipped our rain-diluted tea, interpersonal barriers began to dissolve, and the welcoming smiles of the fishermen managed to melt away even the memories of over-conscientious government officials. On board, the only official was the captain, a short and friendly man who wielded his authority by calling out encouragement through the ship's loudspeaker and signaling with manual gestures meant to time the delicate operations. Later, in the pause before the nets were redeployed, I didn't need Othman's interpretation to understand the gist of what the crewmen were talking about. They pointed to the net and used gestures to echo what their colleagues all around the world were saying over and over again, as if warning, predicting: "No more fish . . . soon!"

A small boat helps to close the purse around a school of sardines. (top)

Sardines dominate the catches of purse seiners. Morocco is the largest canned sardine exporter in the world. (above)

FISH AS MAIN COURSE: CAMBODIA

Most of the boats in Cambodia are small, only about 25 to 30 feet long (8 to 9 meters). I went out on a dragger, taking off from Sihanoukville (Kompong Som) at sunset and spending the night dragging the ocean floor for shrimp and other bottom dwellers. We came in at sunrise; the fishermen sold their catch to wholesalers at the dock. The bycatch, which was enormous, wasn't tossed overboard, but was sold as well, used to make fertilizer or as fish food for aquaculture farms.

Fish and rice are the staples of the Cambodian diet. A great many of the fish eaten in Cambodia arrive either from freshwater sources or from the coasts along the Gulf of Thailand. Cambodia's territorial waters are mostly shallow—no more than 16 feet (50 meters)—and are therefore particularly suitable for trawling.

Hauling and sorting the catch during repetitious dragging for shrimps off the coast of Sihanoukville, Cambodia. (left and above)

Cambodia's fishing potential is underutilized, as most fishermen cannot afford modern, large vessels with which to venture far from shore into the deeper waters and different fisheries of the gulf. Nevertheless, because of the densely populated coast, marine fish stocks are a heavily exploited resource.

Government oversight is sorely lacking and a significant part of the fishing activity is illegal and undocumented, including underreported family-scale fisheries. Moreover, Thai fishing boats regularly cross into Cambodia's Exclusive Economic Zone or load the catches of Cambodian boats. These amounts are also undocumented by Cambodian authorities.

Most Cambodian fishermen cannot afford modern vessels and cannot fish far from shore. (above)

A dragger coming back in at sunrise. (right)

HAND-BAITING HOOKS— LONGLINE FISHING

A THOUSAND STATIONS IN MID-OCEAN: INDIA

I was on the Arabian Sea with no land in sight, amid the waters with Thaddeus, a Tamil fishing captain from southern India. The five crew members started to lower the longline, with its thousand hooks loaded with pieces of shark-baiting oily fish, into the water. Not a word was spoken among them. They lowered the hooks one by one, loosening the longline in what seemed, to me at least, like a chaotic mess of strings—but they saw the underlying order. Gradually, the line of hooks took shape, marking the water's surface with flags that were hoisted on bamboo sticks stuck on buoys.

Chennai (Madras) fishing port

Thaddeus followed the line as it spread out in the water, his eyes already on the flags trying to catch any movements that were unrelated to the breeze. A moment after all the hooks were deployed, he stepped aside and threw up. I picked up an imaginary camera and "clicked." He smiled at me apologetically. "I've been throwing up ever since my first trip on a little boat with my dad." He laughed. "Dad said it would be better for me to become a teacher, so I went to school and became a teacher. But the smell didn't leave me . . . or perhaps it was something else." I offered him one of the patches from my medicine box that you can stick behind your ear to avoid getting sick, but he refused and laughed again. "Do I look like a teacher to you?"

Whose Karma Is Running Out?

As the sun climbed to the top of the sky, Thaddeus and I were sitting together on mattresses (really no more than pieces of cloth as thin as a kitchen towel), leaning against the railing. Thaddeus got up, stretched on deck and hung from a pulley rope dangling overhead, as if testing its strength before the catch came up. He pulled the rope behind him as he sat next to me, playing with its edges and slightly loosening its cords.

"A while ago," he said, throwing the rope behind his shoulder, "maybe yesterday, maybe years ago, we caught this huge shark. So big we couldn't lift it. We dragged it with the boat, or maybe it dragged us, from midnight till morning. There were three of us on the boat, a little open boat. We considered cutting the cord, but you don't give up on such a big fish. Then a big freighter passed. We signaled them and they got closer. They turned their huge crane towards us. We tied the rope and they pulled. A gigantic tiger shark came out of the water. When they dropped it onto our boat, the boat immediately sank below the surface. For a moment, we thought it was the end for us, but then the boat floated back up. The shark weighed 1,400 kilograms" (nearly 3,100 pounds).

"We were lucky." Thaddeus smiled. "But perhaps luck is a matter of karma; you create your own luck, if not in this life, in the next." He then became serious and said, "This shark must have been the last of the giants. I don't know whose karma is running out—ours or the sharks'."

Ninety-nine Percent Pride

The sun rose over Thoothoor Beach, Thaddeus's beach. Thoothoor is a village in southwestern India, part of the Tamil Nadu state. As we approached from the sea, the church spire came into view and the skyline began to jingle with the sounds of bells. A loudspeaker played the Morning Prayer in the local tune as houses came into view, gradually rising out of the sand. Our speed seemed to grow as we approached the dry land. Thaddeus boasted that no other sailboat can brave the breakers of this wide-open beach like the *katumaram*, which nimbly winds its way through the white water.

Despite the early hour, the beach hustled and bustled with activity. A few sailboats approached, repeatedly appearing and disappearing from view as the breakers rose and ebbed. We unloaded our catch, already sorted and packed in nets, to the waiting rafts, which were nothing more than four tree trunks tied together.

After the blues of the open sea, my eyes feasted on the fascinating colors of the saris worn by women out to welcome the fishermen. We got off the boat and waded in the shallows. The loads of beautifully varied colorful fish spread the sand and seemed to warp the space around it as circles of saris began to close in.

"They don't come here because they miss the fishermen," explained Thaddeus. "They are the ones who run the whole show—the prices and who buys what. That's the way it goes here."

A few months after my trip to India, I went on another shark hunt, this time in Australia. There, when I took the photograph of this huge tiger shark, I recalled Thaddeus's story about *his* tiger shark, in the good old days—about twice the size of this one in Australia; I could only imagine what that giant could do to a small boat like Thaddeus's.

No other boat braves the breakers like the *katumaram*—nothing more than four tree trunks tied together. (above)

In the Tamil Nadu region of southern India, women conduct 75 percent of fish commerce. (opposite, top)

Juvenile sharks in an open-air auction. (opposite, bottom)

Indeed, the circles teemed with economic energy as brief auctions were concluded, the results duly noted in a ledger. Cash, so I discovered as I toured the beach, is never exchanged directly in these "fish business" circles. Rather, it is exchanged along their edges, in the ancillary industries that are all part of the trade. Women, for example, crush blocks of ice and sell "snow" by the handful, plate or bowl; other villagers sell tea and fruit at stands; others, porters and packers, are paid to lay out the fresh fish on layers of sand and ice. Farther away, katumaram-builders polish trunks on the sand, shaded by sails stretched on bamboo sticks; still farther, men with their scooters parked in the more reliable shade of the church spires prepare to drive to the nearest marketplace, leaving behind them telltale trails of melting ice.

A few hours passed idly as we waited for the main event. It felt as if things were being purposefully built up to a dramatic climax, but perhaps the cause of this atmosphere was more mundane—the most coveted catch is buried deep within the big boats and therefore takes more time to unload. Thus, it wasn't until noon that the apex predators made their appearance on the beach: Finally, the sharks were brought in.

Sharks are a global commodity. The local shark-fishing industry has not developed in a void, but rather in response to a demand. Sharks, which used to be thrown back into the water as useless bycatch, have become prized for their meat in the local Indian market. Moreover, huge demand for shark fins in East Asia has led to spiraling prices.

On the beach, sharks are the only fish that get weighed. Once the weight is recorded, the fins are cut off. As I walked among the colors I heard people mumbling the English word "export"—the vernacular for fins. Thaddeus, who might have noticed my unease or perhaps anticipated my question, took me by the hand to the fins spread out to dry under the sun for all to see. "Here in Thoothoor," he said, "the sight of the fins shocks no one. It's just another fish part."

The warehouse where the fins are stored at the end of the day is also used to process other parts of the shark catch. Shark meat is cut into slices and covered in a thick layer of raw salt. The liver is dissected and taken to tin barrels where it is heated to produce special oil. In the past, before synthetic substitutes were developed, this oil was used to produce commercial vitamin A. Today, locals use it to coat the boats for waterproofing. Sharkskin is used in the bag industry, the jaws are sold for school displays, and the teeth are sold for jewelry.

Thaddeus had done the math: "We use every gram in the shark's body—well, ninety-nine percent, to be exact." He laughed. My unease did loosen a bit as I thought of that pile of finned sharks I had encountered all those years ago. At least they used all of the shark here.

The people of Thoothoor and twelve other nearby villages became Christian in the mid-sixteenth century, after the Jesuit priest St. Francis Xavier converted ten thousand members of the Mukkuva caste, one of the lowest in the Hindu hierarchy.

Thoothoor's website used to boast that it was a "100 percent Christian village." This label was later removed, but it clearly reflects not only an undeniable demographic fact but also the degree of the church's involvement in the villagers' lives. It charges 5 percent of their revenues to finance its institutions, including the schools that are its pride and joy.

VENTURING OUT IN DANGEROUS WATERS

Appearances can be deceiving. Despite seeming so integral to the local landscape, the shark-fishing traditions of Thoothoor go back no more than a generation or two. Nobody can remember why or how it started, but the villagers began catching sharks only in the late 1980s. By 2000, the fishermen of Thoothoor had built a fleet hundreds of boats strong—the largest deep-sea fishing fleet in the subcontinent.

Throughout history, tough conditions along the Arabian Sea coast have honed the skills of fishermen in India's southern tip. They routinely venture out to distant, dangerous hunting grounds. "We sail from here down south to Gujarat in the north, and arrive at places other fishermen don't dare to reach. We even do it during monsoon storms," boasted Thaddeus.

Prior to the advent of deep-sea fishing, sharks were merely incidental guests in fishing nets cast close to the shoreline. Shark fishing became widespread following a technological revolution that hit the Indian sub-continent like a tidal wave.

Traditional Indian fishing methods were significantly altered by the widespread availability and use of motorized boats and tools. Artisanal fishermen started using their katumarams and dug-out canoes only to ferry their catch to the beach. For fishing, these simple wooden vessels were traded for small motorized boats of plywood or fiberglass that featured specialized designs suited to particular fishing and navigating conditions.

Another aspect of this technological revolution was the introduction of industrial types of fishing; using bigger boats equipped with trawlers dramatically increased fish catches.

Soon, however, due to a lack of planning and supervision, fish populations in shallow waters were depleted, and artisanal fishermen discovered a proportional decline in their earnings. The recent fishing developments have had far-reaching social and economic implications. Artisanal fishermen who were accustomed to managing independent businesses that relied on small and manually controlled boats were forced to deal with big companies and sophisticated fishing equipment that conquered and emptied India's waters.

With their backs to the wall, artisanal fishermen were driven into two courses of action: unionizing and motorizing. Unionizing enjoyed some limited success as fishermen's organizations pressured legislators to create laws that would prohibit fishing with trawlers in waters up to 65 feet (20 meters) deep. Unfortunately, these new laws were never seriously implemented or enforced. Motorizing, on the other hand, has had a profound effect on the industry. The subsequent dwindling of the fish stock forced the skillful artisanal fishermen from the southern end of the Indian subcontinent to rise to the occasion and usher in a new era of deep-sea fishing. Throughout history, they were the few who would sail on long trips in stormy monsoon weather; now they are the ones expanding the horizon of traditional fishing.

From tail to teeth, every part of the shark's body is used.

Good Guys, Bad Guys

Thaddeus's individual story included a chapter of struggle, not against powers of nature, but against "the bad guys," as he put it. With exquisite dramatic skill—perhaps thanks to his experience as a teacher ("I'm the best teacher among the fishermen, but they mock me and say that I'm the best fisherman among the teachers")—he described the day when an Indian coast guard vessel appeared from nowhere and detained one of Thoothoor's fishing boats. "Out of the blue," he said, "from the vessel's loudspeakers, the fishermen first heard about a state law passed several months earlier." They were read a long list of

some sixty species they could no longer fish, including many shark species. Several days later, in a different location, Indian customs authorities stopped the trade in shark fins, and elsewhere they confiscated a cargo of "forbidden" fish on its way from Sri Lanka to the mainland.

The reason for the new restrictions was not clear, and even the state's fishing department heard of it only from the fishermen themselves. When the unions did some research, they found out that the restrictions were the result of a joint initiative by a nongovernmental organization (NGO) and a local environmental magazine. Intoxicated

Fishermen in the fishing port of Chennai, happy to return home after four weeks at sea—and the catch was good.

by the success of a previous campaign against whale shark hunting in Gujarat, far from the fishing grounds of the southern subcontinent, they pushed for the new restrictions. They based their recommendations on a study that had revealed shocking evidence regarding the illegal hunting of sharks for their fins, their bodies thrown back into the water. In the area studied by the NGO, the shark population had been almost completely annihilated.

"The whole thing took place in the Andaman Islands," said Thaddeus, "far away from our waters." Waving his fingers in an angry manner, he added, "This horrible thing is alien to the Thoothoor fishermen's ways in the ocean. We hunt for the fish, not just for the fins."

The new blanket prohibition directly threatened the livelihood of some eight thousand fishermen in Thoothoor and, by extension, about fifty thousand members of their families. Across India, the disputed ban threatened the economic survival of half a million people. For the fishermen of Thoothoor, the regulations could not have been enacted at a worse time. The deep-sea fishing resurgence was at a crucial point in its development. Ironically, the ban itself upset the delicate ecological balance by exposing other smaller species to the now-protected apex predators.

Harsh criticism came from the scientific community and fishing experts alike, who said that the ban was populist and not based on serious research. In fact, scientists who had been carefully monitoring these fishing grounds claimed that the present level of shark fishing was still below the acceptable figures, and that as long as there are no indications of overfishing, there was no reason for a complete ban on fishing sharks. Following months of mass protests and hunger strikes, the ban was finally lifted.

With the same pride with which Thaddeus had pointed to his catch, he told me about SIFFS—the South Indian Federation of Fishermen Societies—an NGO established to protect their collective rights by eliminating mediators, thus allowing the fishermen greater mobility according to market demand. This and other NGOs like it also help bail out fishermen when they get detained or arrested by Indian customs officials, usually at the edge of the country's territorial waters. Dozens have been killed and hundreds injured during violent incidents along the maritime boundary between Sri Lanka and the mainland. Fishermen are often arrested by the coast guards of both countries and jailed for months.

"It takes that long to finish signing all the paperwork," quips Thaddeus. "Come to think of it," he laughs, "if bureaucracy is part of the shark, then we have exploited it one hundred percent, not ninety-nine."

THROUGH THICK AND FINS

For Thoothoor fishermen, even though fins are of precious value, they are nothing more than body parts to be sold along with the rest of their catch, and their value is incommensurable with the traditional value of their craft: shark hunting. Perhaps owing to their pride, Thoothoor fishermen avoid the fin trade and are perhaps unaware of the criminal nature this "export" acquires as it travels away from its home waters and toward their final destination in the markets of Southeast Asia.

I was intrigued, though, and wanted to meet the fin traders.

As expected, the farther I ventured from the indigenous fishermen's hunting grounds, the thicker and more mysterious the intrigue became. I had to use generous amounts of persuasion to obtain the address of a fin "exporter" on the other side of the subcontinent, in the city of Chennai (formerly Madras). I flew there with Asher—my companion through thick and thin. We arrived at a ramshackle building on a busy street. No sign betrayed the nature of the business transacted inside. I knocked on the door.

Suspicious eyes scrutinized us through the narrow opening. In true cloak-and-dagger spirit, I introduced myself as an "American fish merchant." We were led up narrow stairs to an office on the building's top floor. The man behind the desk studied us carefully. I told him about my "American clients" and asked if I could take a look at his factory. He gazed suspiciously at my closed camera bag, but unable to overcome the temptation of a lucrative potential deal, he eventually stood up and led us to the building's sunny roof. There, several women clad in colorful saris toiled among drying lines laden with fins. The fins hung suspended above wicker baskets filled with clumps of dried shark fin fiber glistening golden in the sun. Upon witnessing this scene, I, too, succumbed to temptation. I pulled out my camera, avoiding Asher's alert hands as he tried to stop me.

Out of the blue, two men pounced on us and pushed us down the stairs. As I imagined myself disappearing "under mysterious circumstances," I had an inspiration and instinctively pulled out my "credentials": the *Sharks!* book I always carry in my camera bag in lieu of a calling card. As I held it up, I shouted, *"National Geographic!"* This seemed to do the trick. I handed the book to the man behind the desk and said, "I'm a photographer, that's me, this is mine!" as I pointed to my name on the cover. The man froze for a second, then eased up and smiled. Obviously my desperate tactic had worked; he was impressed. "Why didn't you tell me from the start? I would have let you take all the pictures you want," he said. But then he opened the book and looked at the author photograph showing the young man I used to be, not the much heavier and older man I had become. Immediately he tensed again and gave me a lethal look. "But that's not you," he said. "I don't believe a word you're saying." He shoved the book under his armpit and shouted, "Out, right now!"

WHAT WILL BE LEFT FOR THE NEXT GENERATION? THE AZORES

I joined Captain Pacheco on board his boat, the *Alda Maria*. He was only twenty-three years old. With him were his fifteen-year-old brother and four older male family members. We were setting out from Ponta Delgada, the main fishing port on São Miguel Island, in the Azores. The Azores are an archipelago of volcanic islands in the Atlantic Ocean, west of Portugal. The islands rise in sharp cliffs above the mid-oceanic ridge where three tectonic plates—the North American, Eurasian, and African—collide. All of the fishermen aboard the *Alda Maria*, including Captain Pacheco (no connection to the Pacheco who captained my Cocos Island dives) came from the small fishing village of Ponta dos Carneiros, 8 miles (12 kilometers) from Ponta Delgada.

Pacheco's family members rushed to and fro across the deck, letting down a 6.5-mile (10 kilometer) longline equipped with 7,000 hooks. It was a special kind of longline designed to lie very deep, all the way down along the ocean floor. The men worked within the small confines of the boat at an impressively frantic pace to get the hooks set. There was a special, easygoing camaraderie among the crew. They worked together like a well-oiled machine.

It was a rare, quiet night amid the stormy winter. "Quiet" is a relative term, of course, as the sea was still quite choppy and it rained relentlessly, but it was the first navigable night in three weeks.

The crew worked through the night. By 5AM, they had laid down all the hooks and baits, and Captain Pacheco had turned the wheel around. We headed back, following the longline toward shore. Only then did the fishermen find time to catnap on deck.

To best position the longline, the fishermen used all the state-of-the-art technology they had at their disposal: electronic depth-finders, colored computer graphics of the ocean floor, and GPS. Despite all this technological sophistication, however, it was impossible to foresee what the 7,000 hooks would seize. And when they started hauling in the catch, nobody could explain why the first fifty were completely bereft of fish, while the next twenty each were laden with a marvelous creature of the deep—the silver scabbardfish.

I was amazed by the skill these fishermen possess. In fast, fluid movements, they removed the fish from the hooks with their hand poles and dropped them into a plastic container.

Midnight in Ponta Delgada port: the *Alda Maria* before going out to the stormy sea. (opposite)

Captain Pacheco, *right,* **and his family of fishermen**—two generations aboard the boat. (above)

At 4PM, they pulled into port and off-loaded their catch. The captain's father was there to meet the boat, and the fourteen-hour fishing day ended. It would all begin again in just ten short hours.

The young Captain Pacheco knows that the longer the spells of his breaks from fishing, the more fish he catches. And when he looks at the big boats that often trespass into his territory, some of them illegally, he also understands the same simple math: The more fish you catch, the fewer are left for next time. But Captain Pacheco cannot wait days between voyages—he has a family to provide for. For this reason, and maybe others, the fishery is dwindling. Pacheco wonders what he will be left with when his brother becomes a captain . . . and what will be left for the next generation.

Sorting the catch after the long(lining) night. (opposite)

A short catnap and break before hauling in the catch. (left, top and bottom)

Scabbard fish: their reflective eyes have adjusted to the scarce light in the abyss in which they live. (right)

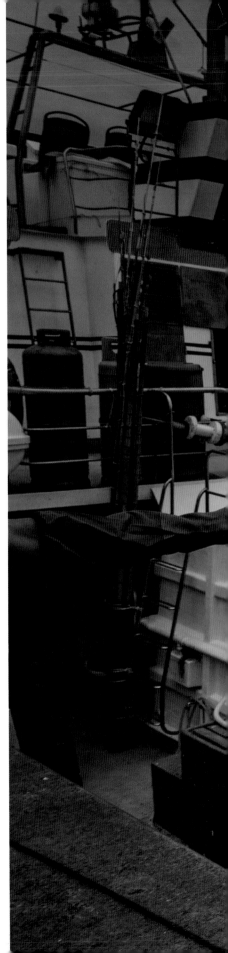

More than 222 pounds (100 kilos) of yellowfin tuna being moved to an auction house for export. Most of the Azore people cannot afford their price. (top left)

Deep bottom sharks caught on longlines and brought to Ponta Delgada, the main fishing port on San Miguel Island. (bottom left)

Yellowfin tuna being off-loaded from the boat; most of the catch is exported to Europe. (right)

FOLLOWING TRADITION— ARTISANAL FISHING

WAR WAS GOOD FOR THE FISH: MOZAMBIQUE

A Bit of Ice for the Road

"If you want to know something about fishing in Mozambique," said Antonio as we boarded his traditional dhow sailboat, "you must begin with what happens on land."

I had been looking for a boat to take me out from the fishing town of Xai-Xai (pronounced "shy-shy") in southern Mozambique. I was hooked by the wide smile Antonio gave me, as if he knew me or saw something I could not see.

Dhow—a traditional sailing boat used in the Indian Ocean region.

Ice shortages and lack of cold storage facilities cause high post-harvest losses.

As fate would have it, his words proved prophetic. On my very first day, bending under the sail, I was paralyzed by a terrible backache that always seems to flare up on me in the wrong time and place. I wondered what I had done to bring on this bad luck. With all the superstitions I've been collecting (and adopting) over the years, I almost feel like I've turned into a fisherman. New superstitions do not supersede older ones, they are just added to the others. Fishing boats hang for dear life between heaven and the deep, so why *not* try to avoid thinking about storms? Why *not* avoid whistling on deck so as not to summon the winds? Storms and winds can bring devastation, so you might as well do what you can do keep them at bay. The same reasoning prohibits taking bananas, women, and suitcases on deck—each thought to welcome bad luck at sea. Only the devil knows why sailing on Friday is such a taboo or why urinating on a new net is considered good luck, but they are, and so the fishermen avoid Fridays and always piss on the new nets.

Anyway, the only cures for my back problem were to lie motionless for two weeks or get an injection right where it hurts. "We have to drive to Maputo," Antonio told me. "It's the only place where you could get a shot like that."

The highway connecting Maputo, the capital of Mozambique, to the northern coastal towns made perfectly clear what Antonio had meant about the land dictating what happens at sea. He voiced what I had inferred: "Try transporting fish on a road such as this, especially when you have no ice to preserve them with." Indeed, the trip felt like an endless series of bumps and holes, and we had to endure many long traffic back-ups caused by incoming traffic and stuck vehicles. Antonio saw me squirming in agony next to him, and said by way of apology, "It will take some time before the country recovers from the war—but we are on the right track." He laughed. "It was a disaster for us but at least it was good for the fish."

I didn't laugh. In fact, I wasn't sure I even understood. He explained that the infrastructure destruction during the fifteen-year civil war limited the fishermen's ability to fish. As a result, the fish prospered. But things didn't get much better for the fishermen after the war ended. Political upheavals not only prevented any effective oversight of fishing regulations, they also slowed the recovery of the shattered infrastructure.

"We still don't have enough ice factories to enable us to fish more than one day's journey away from the beach," said Antonio, "and certainly not to move them inland once they're caught. The result is that you fish only the amount your family and your customers can eat at once, before the fish stinks, so you don't fish much in the first place. You can ask the fish." He laughed again and repeated his sad joke. "The war was good for the fish."

Biting a Fish Tale

After I concluded my painful business in Maputo, Antonio agreed to be my guide and take me on a driving tour up the coast. We headed north, passing through fishing towns along the western coast of the Indian Ocean. Wherever we stopped, I talked to the fishermen and they echoed Antonio's claim that they were hardly getting by, that their catches were meager. Yet I kept photographing fishermen unloading bountiful nets. And when I read a research article about the fishing in Mozambique, I got confused. The scientific sources suggested a huge gap between the catch figures that the fishermen report and reality—far more fish are being caught than are being reported. The fishermen's figures are anecdotal, claimed the scientist, and cannot be used as a basis for serious plans for oversight and infrastructural development.

When I asked Antonio about this gap, he shrugged and said: "What we fish immediately disappears in people's stomachs. Go figure," he said with a laugh. "It leaves

In Mozambique's southern region, women are involved in commercial fishing and also work in the markets.

us penniless," he continued acrimoniously. "Many fishermen don't even have boats. All they can do is seine fishing with nets on the beach. Some use illegal *chicocota* nets with holes the size of mosquito nets. The net leaves nothing in the water and most of the catch is thrown back dead—but at least it puts something on their plates."

I asked him whether it was only lack of funds that kept him from putting a motor on his boat. He shrugged again, but then said, "Even if the government gave us motors for free, and other things, such as large nets and ice, we would still need a lot of money on top to take advantage of such gifts—to buy fuel, for example." Pointing out to the horizon, he continued, "They give licenses to foreign boats to fish in our deep sea, where we cannot reach."

When I talked to Antonio about these foreign fleets, I realized that although the colonial powers of the Portuguese were long gone, the feelings of exploitation were still very present. Antonio explained that the huge ships, many of them European, Japanese, and Chinese, operate as floating territories unto themselves—foreign powers stirring the oceans and reaping its treasures. With cooled storage spaces that can carry an ocean of fish, and with an ocean of time to spare, these boats operate completely independent of the ice clock that governs the lives of all those fishermen who operate on small boats.

But then Antonio broke into a big smile. "People on those huge monsters don't see their families for three months. A friend of mine used to work on such a ship and told me that they don't even smell like a fishing boat." He laughed. "My friend looked for a bucket to relieve himself, and all the people there laughed at him. 'Those poor workmen,' my friend said, 'they eat in shifts, shit in shifts—hell, they even snore in shifts, like a bloody orchestra.'"

"It's not only the foreigners," Antonio admitted. "When the war ended, fish heaven ended too. Ever since the war we have more fishermen, more boats, more families to feed, more chaos, and less and less fish. In the end, you will find fish only in hotels and fancy restaurants." He laughed bitterly, "Many tourists have been coming here recently, mostly divers. And tourists want to see fish on their dinner plates—but, God forbid, not the beautiful fish they have met underwater in the morning." I nodded guiltily and thought, How ironic: If it weren't for my backache, I, too, would find time, between fishing trips, to dive in those glorious waters with my beloved mantas and whale sharks, taking photographs that would make them famous. To humor him, I told Antonio about a scandal that broke

A **twelve-man crew** goes out to set the beach seine in early morning. (above)

For local consumption, sharks are sold fresh and preserved by sun, drying, and smoking. (opposite)

out when some fishermen gutted manta rays and sharks on the beach, right in front of flabbergasted tourists. One commentator protested against this threat to the emerging tourism industry. "Indeed," I said, "no one wants to see blood on their plate."

Perhaps the images I captured on this trip, of fishermen with bulging nets, were also only anecdotal, just a question of luck. Maybe these anecdotes become fish tales among fishermen: Like a fish biting its own tail, these sporadic catches are like bait, luring fishermen to keep trying their luck in hope that somehow good luck will change the reality. Lucky for me, I thought, I fished this wonderful, bittersweet Antonio out of the Mozambican ocean.

A shovelnose shark caught by gill net; the underside of this bottom-feeder looks like a giant skate with a tail. (top left)

At 3AM, fishermen as young as fourteen row their boat, dragging the net through the tidal shallows. (bottom left)

Women and children form a substantial part of the fisheries without boats, and constitute the majority of collectors. Here, villagers pull the beach seine on Sunday morning. (right)

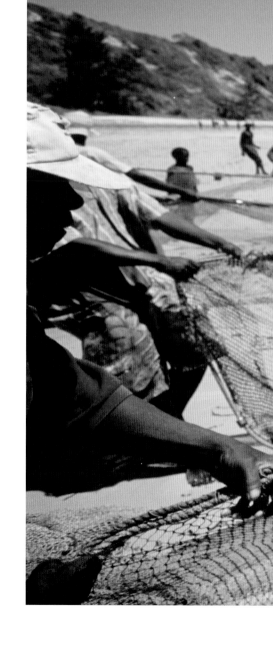

WHOSE TURTLES ARE THESE?
MISKITO CAYS

Sleeping Rocks

George had invited me to sail in "our *duritara*," a sailboat—one of the last to brave this ocean with nothing but wind to power it. George was the senior fisherman aboard. From its deck, we could see some shacks that appeared to hang in the air above the horizon, no sign of land around them. A light wind pushed us slowly across the calm water towards the shacks. As we approached, clouds rose in the distance and the shacks seemed to be sailing on the sky's reflection of the water. Only when we got close enough to make out the faces of people inside them did I notice the stilts anchoring the wooden shacks to the ocean's bottom.

We had arrived at the Miskito Cays, an archipelago that comprises a variety of formations: estuaries, coral reefs, cays, sea grass beds, and islets. Here, in the Caribbean waters about 25 miles (40 kilometers) from mainland Nicaragua, the firm soil is out of sight. A unique community of Miskito Indians, an ethnic group native to Central America, had built wooden houses on stilts, erected above the water. These shacks form a kind of makeshift village that serves as a mid-ocean haven for the fishermen. The trip to the best fishing spots from the Miskito Coast along the eastern edge of Nicaragua and Honduras takes several hours, even when the wind is good. It's too far to go there and back in the same day so the fishermen stay in the shacks, sometimes for months at a time.

The people who welcomed us that afternoon looked worryingly at the sky. Rain clouds were forming above the horizon, covering the sun as it was about to set. "You have brought the storm with you," they said in a mock scolding tone.

A duritara—one of the last sailing boats in this part of the ocean.

A makeshift village in mid-ocean creates a haven for the Miskito turtle fishermen.

Before the sun set, we rushed to head out to a group of "sleeping rocks"—their term for the coral outcrops that large juvenile and adult green and hawksbill turtles visit at night. We laid large mesh gill nets on the rocks and anchored them in place using the heaviest coral heads we could find, lest the nets be carried away by the currents, winds, or the spasms of our prey as it fought for dear life.

We sailed back toward the shacks. The wind grew stronger and blew directly into our faces. We had to tack all the way back, and arrived when it was already dark. The storm was polite enough to wait until we had installed three plastic sheets to protect the shacks from three possible directions of this horror. Once the storm started, nothing diminished the wind and rain flying over the open ocean, so it battered the "walls" of our shacks fiercely. I buried myself deep inside my sleeping bag and for an interminable night, listened to the rain as it beat the roof. Water filtered through, and heavy drops landed on top of me.

At first light we got quickly to our feet, only too happy to leave our wet sleeping bags. When we reached the sleeping rocks, nobody was surprised to find empty nets, nor was anybody surprised that some of the nets were gone, others torn. But George smiled and said, "Our next night can only be better." The sky was already bright, and the wind subsided as we sailed out to more distant sleeping rocks that had not been frequented by fishermen in a long while. But the price of sailing quietly in the wind was paid in time spent—hours passed before we got to our destination and spread our nets.

That night, back in our shack but this time under calm skies, the collection of shelters became a "place," somewhere suitable for sleeping and cooking, somewhere worthy of a name: Wiplin—"our Wiplin," George called it. We built an open fire using mangrove firewood brought from the mainland or collected at the distant cays. The wood was arranged on the metal top of a fifty-gallon oil drum that had been brought just for this purpose. Cornmeal or flour was used to make something that resembled bread. Salt was our only spice; there wasn't even sugar for the coffee. But there were a few cans of pineapple, and some rice and beans. After almost two days without food, my hunger turned these far-from-appetizing items to delicacies; the sounds of my surroundings added a priceless spice to the bland food. I walked out and stood on the deck connecting the two shacks, listened to the water moving under me like an endless river, and floated between worlds in this "place/non-place"—not land, not sea, not even boat.

The next morning, we sailed to the sleeping rocks again. The wind dictated our speed, but the men still stared at the sails as if their gazes could encourage them to propel us faster. They were clearly tense—having pulled in nothing but empty nets for a week before George and I arrived.

Everyone was relieved when we pulled the first gill net and came up with a green turtle. The other nets had also caught turtles: a loggerhead, a hawksbill, and four other green turtles. Two of the greens were adults, and required several hands to haul them on

The cays have no potable water or electricity. Water is brought from the coast in boats. (top)

A fisherman cooks a turtle using mangrove firewood collected with boats. (bottom)

board. The men looked at me, and I put my camera down and joined hands with them. My partners made sure I had a good grasp on the two front flippers, and then all together let go. For a moment I was heady with pride for being able to carry the turtle's unbelievable weight, until a sharp pain in my back overcame me, and I let go. The turtle, still entangled in the net, fell into the water and I followed suit; my pride was hurt but my back was saved. These backaches of mine had already put an end to a few very expensive voyages in the farthest ends of the world. The idea of having to lie flat on the bottom of a sailboat all the way back to the mainland horrified me. I got back on the boat, but not before the men recaptured the turtle. A while later I was finally able to join the fishermen's laughter.

The turtles were placed belly up inside the hull of the boat. After a week away from family and friends, with the lonely huts at Wiplin as their only refuge, the fishermen, with their boatload of sea turtles, could finally return home.

Our Wind, Our Waters, Our Turtles

We turned the duritara back toward the fishermen's home in Sandy Bay, a tropical river and lagoon system in Nicaragua surrounded by ten Miskito communities. The wind had died down almost completely and we had to sail through the night to get home; we just sat there for eight hours till a small breeze mercifully came up and pushed us along.

When we reached the narrow river close to the men's houses, the heat from the morning sun was already intense. We pulled the duritara close to the riverbank and started to off-load. Family and friends arrived to help carry the equipment and catch to shore. First, the nets, cooking utensils, knives, and other gear were thrown over the side of the boat to the riverbank. Then, ropes were tied around each turtle's front flippers and the turtles were hauled overboard. They landed with a splash, trapped on their backs in the shallow river. The turtles thrashed in vain as men held the ropes firmly. Eventually, they grew still. Then they were pulled up on the grassy slope next to the river and laid on their backs. Occasionally, we heard a deep breath as a turtle struggled to inhale air, its body unaccustomed to the lack of buoyancy on land.

A customer sized up one turtle and purchased it. An adult green turtle can supply plenty of food. After fish, turtle meat is the cheapest source of protein on the Caribbean coast of Nicaragua. It is a staple.

Later, George took me to his home. I was offered turtle meat, and couldn't resist my

Miskito fishermen target specific animals out of a wide variety of seemingly available species. (opposite)

Although many Miskito villages have access to both shallow offshore waters and tropical rainforest environments, 65 percent of the fishermen concentrate solely on turtle fishing. (above)

curiosity. It was one of the best meats I've ever tasted, very fatty and delicious, reminding me of an exquisite rack of lamb, only better.

After this lunch break, George was eager to show me something, as if to make a point. He took me back to the river slope and looked for something on the bodies of the still-living turtles. He carefully checked each one's flippers until he found what he was looking for—a small badge. Triumphantly, he pointed to it and said, "This one came from Tortuguero Coast in Costa Rica. They can say whatever they want, but these turtles are ours." Only then did I realize that, perhaps provocatively, he referred to everything that had to do with his corner of the ocean as "our"—from the wind that blows the sails of his boat ("our wind") to the tiniest of turtles caught in his gill net. Perhaps I, the stranger, was the only one who heard any provocation—it sounded perfectly natural to all the rest. "Our waters" are not political and have nothing to do with any local or international legal definition; "our waters" is the inheritance of generations—from horizon to horizon—all the fish and turtles ever caught in the net and all those still to be brought upon the boat with which the fisherman plows his waters.

When I asked George who "they" were, he said, "They in Tortuguero. They think this their turtle because born there, but he eats in our waters. It is our turtle." George smiled. "We Miskito, and this Miskito Beach."

Meat—particularly turtle meat—is the single most sought after food and is the center of interest in Miskito villages. (left)
Sailing into the night to get back home. (opposite)

A GIANT IN THE DARK: TORTUGUERO, COSTA RICA

We were running along the black sand beach in almost complete darkness. The abundant driftwood, along with everything from plastic bottles to strands of water hyacinth, made it a hazardous endeavor. Adding to the challenge were my stiff legs and my heavy backpack full of equipment.

I got to Tortuguero, the "land of turtles," after my fishing trip with George. Tortuguero is both a village and national park in Costa Rica. I made the trip to document researchers and volunteers tagging some of the turtles that hatch on their sands. We had been waiting for hours crouched under a tarp to hide from the pounding rain when we finally got the call we had been hoping for all night—one of the patrol teams reported by radio that a leatherback turtle was in the process of digging an egg chamber roughly a mile from where we were stationed.

We had to get to the turtle before it started to lay its eggs. Our objective was to attach a harness with a satellite transmitter to its leathery shell—no mean feat. The leatherback is the largest of all the world's sea turtles and the carapace of the females that come ashore to nest at Tortuguero measure about 5 feet (1.5 meters). Add a large head, long flippers, and a short tail and you have an animal as long as an outstretched human but weighing five times as much.

Leatherback turtles spend almost their entire lives in the ocean. The only time that researchers have easy access to these marine giants is when the females crawl onto remote tropical and subtropical beaches to dig nests and lay their eggs. The turtles' huge size prevents them from nesting during the day when the unrelenting sunshine would cause lethal overheating. Instead, they emerge under the cover of darkness to perform a primeval nesting ritual that lasts an hour or two.

We arrived at the scene. The international team of researchers from the nonprofit Caribbean Conservation Corporation (today known as the Sea Turtle Conservancy) began preparing while the leatherback turtle completed her excavation of the egg chamber in a determined fashion. Once the female turtle stopped moving her rear flippers, the research team began the frantic fifteen-minute process of applying the harness. When she finished laying her eggs, the leatherback moved her rear fins to fill in the egg chamber. A short time afterwards, she threw sand over the nest with powerful strokes of her long front flippers.

Nesting completed, the turtle crawled back toward the sea. The giant leatherback disappeared through the breaking waves into her ocean home, leaving behind eighty eggs buried in the sand.

LIKE SHARKS, FISHERMEN CANNOT GO BACKWARDS: SEA OF CORTEZ, MEXICO

Today, No One Can Afford to Be Picky

The sun set over us as we went out on Conejo's small fiberglass *panga* in the Sea of Cortez. Conejo is one of an estimated 4,500 *pangeros,* small-boat fishermen who set their gill nets in the long narrow gulf that stretches over 620 miles (1,000 kilometers) south of the Arizona border to the tip of Baja California Sur. Conejo was using two gigantic outboard engines to speed across the water surface far away from the coast. As the moon rose, Conejo spread the gill net and pointed at the water. Just below the surface, a loose school of giant mantas, some as wide as 10 feet (nearly three meters), swam through clouds of post-larval rosado shrimp. Their mouths perpetually open, the big rays glided along, propelled by the smooth flapping of their powerful wings. One dove and then rocketed up, breaking the surface and flapping once in the air before splashing back into the sea.

Shrimp rise to surface at night, and the mantas had followed the moving feast, oblivious to the fishermen's nets. The shrimp larvae passed easily through the 8-inch (20-centimeter) mesh, but three of the big manta hit the net in a quick succession. As soon as the first felt the lines touch its body, it reacted violently, twisting and thrashing. Every turn, however, only wound it more tightly into the net. The wings tried to flap, but what was grace-in-motion just moments before now became clumsy. After several minutes of struggling, it hung exhausted in the tangled mesh. Its two companions didn't fare any better.

"Sharks and mantas cannot go backwards," said Conejo.

Following the shrimp as they rise toward the surface at night, mantas become caught in the fishermen's net. (right)

Sliding this giant manta (also called a "devil ray") into the boat requires considerable joint effort. (opposite)

In the afternoon, we arrived at the beach. As the sun lowered, members of Conejo's family, mostly older men, arrived. "Every year," Conejo said, "fewer young people follow us parents to the fishing life. That's fine with me—I would rather see my children in school." As he prepared his boat, Conejo puffed his chest with pride. "My daughter is a university-educated engineer. You see, I wasn't born a fisherman. Before I became a fisherman I was a crocodile hunter, deep inland, and then a man killed my grandmother. My grandfather shot him." He raised an imaginary rifle to his shoulder. "We thought they would get us—revenge—so my family escaped to the Sea of Cortez, and I became a fisherman."

Conejo sat down and pulled out a knife to cut one of the lines that had tangled. He passed the blade over the palm of his hand, assessing its sharpness. "Nobody chases you in the water," he said. "Only luck. We fishermen will empty the sea down to the last worm, but will always think it's all about luck."

The primary target in this fishery is shark fin, although the wings of mantas are a very significant food source. Conejo referred to manta as a bycatch. "Huge mantas are just for tourists to take pictures," said Conejo. "But today, no one can afford to be picky." He added, "A fisher must fish."

You Can't Blame Us Fishermen

I went out with Conejo to hunt sharks during the peak of the thresher shark-fishing season, which coincides with their pupping season. Threshers have only two to four pups at a time. Such low fecundity makes them extremely vulnerable to overfishing. Cutting embryonic sharks out of the womb occurs often enough that the unborn animals have a market name, *cazon,* and fetch $2 a kilogram. "They make great *ceviche*," said Conejo.

Many fishermen in these waters take advantage of aggregations that form for spawning, casting their gill nets in the fish's assembly areas precisely when they are about to reproduce. Spawning is absolutely critical to the continuing lifecycle, so the removal of ready-to-spawn individuals from the ecosystem has proved disastrous to the renewal of fish populations in the Sea of Cortez.

When I pointed out that these fishing practices must be a huge problem for the threshers, he shrugged and then agreed. "Yes, you can see it when you go to the market. All the fish keep getting smaller. The ones you see today used to be thrown overboard like garbage." But Conejo had no trouble redirecting the blame: "I know a lot of fishermen who work without a license." With an ambiguous smile, he added, "They mostly fish at night to avoid getting caught, although you don't see any wardens at daytime either."

The Mexican government has enacted some regulations, declaring several areas closed to fishing, and banning the use of gill nets and trawlers in others. But because of their huge size, and a lack of manpower to enforce the rules, the fishing areas are almost impossible to police effectively. Thousands of fishing boats operate illegally, so many that unlicensed fishermen catch almost half the fish in Mexico.

Conejo laughed. "But you can't blame us fishermen. For the boat to be legit you have to carry so much paperwork there's no room for the fish." He shrugged and continued, "I understand what all this will do to the future of fishermen, to the future of this sea, but I got to live. I must pay for the fuel—seven, eight, nine pesos a liter—for rice, and what not. . . . What would they have us do, use sail boats?" Always the aphorist, he ended by repeating, "A fisherman gotta fish." As his companions nodded in agreement, he added, "Like sharks, we fishermen cannot go backwards."

Fishermen prefer to catch sharks for their high-priced fins. (opposite, top)

Finning sharks—the first thing fishermen do upon arrival at the beach. (opposite, center)

Embryonic thresher sharks are used in ceviche, a popular Mexican seafood dish. (opposite, bottom)

All the strength that evolution has bred in the sharks works against them; they twist and thrash until the net binds them tight—and they die there. (right)

COLORS CAUGHT IN THE NET: RED SEA

Thanks to the Sea

Even after I had turned my photography focus to fishing, I continued to travel between my home port in New England, and my other home on the Red Sea. Abu Sneida, the Bedouin fisherman with whom I had been sailing the waters of the Red Sea for more than thirty years, headed his tiny wooden felucca towards Ras Muhammad. The veteran fisherman's radar eyes navigated us safely among the reefs that line the coasts of the Sinai Peninsula and the bays of the Red Sea.

"Thanks to the sea," said Abu Sneida, "the Mazeina, our tribe, has never had to leave this spot. All the rest came and went whenever there was famine or war or some other catastrophe. But," he smiled, "we have been here since the time of Nebbi Musa—Moses the Prophet. This sea belongs to us, to the Mazeina." Gesturing towards the great sea, he added, "We sail from the southern tip of Sinai along the entire coast of Saudi Arabia, and from Egypt down to the Horn of Africa, and we have been doing it since time immemorial. We live by it."

The Bedouins hunt in the two gulfs that extend northeast and northwest of here, along the two sea-locked sides of the Sinai triangle: the Gulf of Aqaba (Eilat) and the Gulf of Suez. Structurally, the two are very different. The Gulf of Aqaba, which is geologically younger, is a sharp, deep rift in the Earth's crust, some 5,900 feet (1,800 meters) deep. The Gulf of Suez, on the other hand, is much shallower. In certain sections, it is shallow enough to make sense of the Biblical story about the Children of Israel crossing it on foot while on the run from Pharaoh's hosts. From the tip of the peninsula, the Red Sea stretches southwards for some 1,200 miles (2,000 kilometers) to the Bab al-Mandeb Strait, where it joins the Indian Ocean. The Red Sea is a huge rift separating the African and Arabian tectonic plates, which are continuously pulling away from each other. At the present rate—15 miles (25 kilometers) every million years—it will take many millions of years for this sea to become a veritable ocean, but Abu Sneida will surely still be here.

Abu Sneida straightened his bent back a bit and lifted the net from the felucca's bottom. I was surprised by the small size of the mesh holes. Holes that small do not filter out younger fish, but instead clean out the entire reef, leaving a lifeless desert behind. I had never seen him use this type of net.

I know this reef well; I've been here countless times, admiring and documenting its beauty. I have also seen how it has changed throughout the years, becoming more and more like the inhospitable mountains that tower over the waters. I wanted to say something, to protest, but I couldn't. It was not for me to make judgments on that boat.

Spreading gill nets on the coral reef minutes before dark.

Peacock grouper,
Red Sea, Egypt
(top left)

Squaretail grouper
(top) **and blackback
butterflyfish,
Red Sea, Egypt**
(bottom left)

The gill net caught
a variety of small
reef fish including
goatfish and
parrotfish in the
Gordon Reef, Straits
of Tiran, Red Sea,
Egypt. (right)

FOR A PLATE OF FISH

The Sinai coasts, particularly along the southern tip, are under enormous development pressures driven by the tourist industry. The momentum has completely changed the nature of the area. Before its conquest by Israel in 1967, Sharm al-Sheikh was a small fishing village, which was quickly transformed into a popular tourist destination. A second, more significant boost in development occurred following the return of the Sinai Peninsula to Egyptian sovereignty in 1982. At that time, the Ras Muhammad area was declared a nature reserve called the Ras Muhammad National Park System. Regulations to protect the coral reef were enacted, including a complete ban on fishing within the reserve, and severely restricted fishing in adjacent areas. By 1995, Sharm al-Sheikh was a vital tourist center boasting some forty luxury hotels, thirty-two diving clubs, and hundreds of large safari boats tied up in the harbor.

During those transformative years, the Red Sea's fishing industry evolved to include engine-powered boats and more efficient fishing equipment. Trawlers were introduced in the Suez Gulf area, substantially increasing catch volumes. The demand for fish, both due to the natural growth of the Egyptian population and even faster growth in the tourist population (at least during the peaceful days prior to the political turmoil in Egypt), spurred unsustainable fishing that depleted the fishery in both the Gulf of Aqaba and the Gulf of Suez. Consequently, Egyptian fishermen from the western coast of the Red Sea were forced to look for alternative hunting grounds. They arrived at the South Sinai reef, the traditional tribal areas of the Mazeinas—Abu Sneida's tribe.

The competition over the dwindling fishery has often led to clashes between the Mazeinas of Sinai Peninsula and fishermen from the Egyptian mainland. In an attempt to protect their traditional hunting grounds, the Bedouins act to banish the aliens, sometimes cutting their nets or deliberately tangling them in their boat engines. Both groups, however, find it difficult to adjust to the strict regulations in the preservation area. The government's attempt to protect the reef and preserve it for tourists is counterbalanced by the growing demand for fresh fish, which is ironically fueled by the tourist industry.

Tourist development causes additional damage, both direct and indirect, to the sensitive ecosystem of the reef. Allocating open areas along the coast to construction has come at the expense of turtle nesting grounds and habitats of other creatures, both flora and fauna. Intense lobbying by various environmental organizations has provided many measures of protection to the reef, however, including the prohibitions on filling the reef with sand to create private beaches

and on pouring sewage into the gulf. Without these prohibitions in place, the reef might have already been made history. But even strict regulations and intensive oversight cannot prevent the stress regularly experienced by all living creatures on the reef because of the intense traffic of human bodies and vessels.

It is also impossible to assess the shock and damage caused by the heavy engineering equipment used to build the infrastructures for hundreds of thousands of tourists, employees in the tourist industries, government officials, and soldiers—most of whom come from afar, from Egypt's overcrowded megalopolises in the Nile Valley, or from Northern Sinai. All these factors join to threaten the delicate ecological balance of this unique habitat.

To these long-term factors we must add the short-term damage caused by the thousands of divers who frequent the reef every day—those for whom the nature reserve is protected. A study found that each of those divers contacts the reef corals an average of eight times per dive. Half those contacts cause irreversible damage to the brittle corals. This damage starts a chain reaction, affecting all the flora and fauna in the reef area.

Abu Sneida knew he was breaking the law. He cannot fish there and cannot use such a net. But he does not feel that this state law is his law. In his memory, which encompasses the memories of all generations since the dawn of time, many hostile tribes, conquerors, and rulers have passed through here. The legacy of his forefathers governs this land and these waters—not the government. This is why he lets me photograph. He trusts me to ensure that these memories will be perpetuated. For the last thirty years, he has been accompanying me in my trips, sharing diving boats with me, his own felucca, his meals, whenever I come to visit. And together, over thirty years, we have witnessed the transformation of these waters.

Heroes of Tradition

Personally, I was a witness to the painful change in these waters. Until the early 1980s, Ras Muhammad was world-renowned for shark sightings, especially for the Christmastime appearance of whitetip reef sharks. Each year, around Christmas, hundreds of whitetips would congregate to mate. It lasted for only about two weeks, but what a sight! As far as I know, that scene was last observed in 1982.

My eyes have seen schools of 110-pound (50-kilogram) dogtooth tuna cruise within a few feet of me as I clung to Ras Muhammad's famous vertical wall. I could almost reach out and touch them, they came that close. But if you intend to go there yourself, have no fear of these giant fish: I haven't seen even a tiny dogtooth tuna there in more than twenty years.

"Where are all the big predators? Why are there no sharks, mantas, or turtles? Where are the groupers and the schools of parrotfish that used to pass in endless trains?" I asked Abu Sneida—rhetorically, of course. "You must also remember," replied Abu Sneida, "how around April, on moonlit nights, the *shuri* (red-spotted emperor fish) used to come here in never-ending schools." Gesturing towards the sea in a movement that seemed to engulf it all, he added, "Where are they now? Either they don't come at all or they come in little handfuls that you can put inside one pocket." Abu Sneida returned his hand to the wheel and directed the felucca back to shore. "If you can't rely on the *shuri*, you can't rely on anything anymore."

I once found a book about the Bedouins on a divers' boat. In it, I read about encounters between Bedouins—the desert-dwelling Arabian people—and the inhabitants of distant African coasts, about the African myths that have been blended into their culture. Normally, it is easy to get fish tales out of Abu Sneida, but when I ask him about the spirits and demons of the sea, he falls silent.

I know the extent to which Bedouins, mainly desert nomads, are in awe of the elements, but that alone doesn't explain Abu Sneida's silence. I believe that when talking to strangers, it is difficult for him to admit the inherent contradiction between pagan

legends of oceanic demons and his Islamic faith, which strictly forbids any form of idolatry.

It takes a very long night, usually one involving music and dance with his fellow fishermen, to loosen his tongue. Once loosened, if I'm lucky, it becomes unstoppable. On one night like this he shared a bit of his folklore with me. Abu Sneida's sea takes the form of an abstract divine figure who embraces a variety of different creatures, such as the nymph Hurriya. Hurriya is a sort of benevolent deity even though she claims poor fishermen, like Abu Sneida's brother, and takes them to her abysmal abode. Another creature, Iblis, on the other hand, is the infamous leader of sea demons. He harasses fishermen by conjuring local storms to suddenly and violently rock their boats, stealing their baits and catches, and releasing predators such as sharks and barracudas upon them.

After that night, in the moment of transition between night and day, between greenish-gray and blue, between the occult and the divine, Abu Sneida stepped aside to pray. The rest of his friends followed suit. The same skies protect them all, though under different guises and appellations. But not me. I feel naked, exposed. I guess, after all, I'm not a true believer.

Bottlenose dolphin, Sinai Peninsula, Egypt Dolphins are complex, curious creatures that often interact with humans. A unique "friendship" developed between Abdallah, a deaf Bedouin fisherman, and this dolphin named Oleen who lived with him in Nuewaba, Sinai. Oleen was so comfortable with Abdullah that she even nursed her baby there.

EPILOGUE

THE
LAST
FISHERMAN

My voyage started in New England, but I want to end it in my second home: the Red Sea. I was with Abu Sneida once again, as he piloted his felucca toward one of several yachts. His son is the yacht's captain. Not one of Abu Sneida's twelve children is a fisherman. Two of them have managed to obtain licenses and pilot divers' yachts—these are the only ones still attached to the sea.

Abu Sneida tied his felucca to the far more magnificent vessel. His son showed up on deck, towering above us. He asked if we had brought some fish. "It's for the tourists," he explained. "They want something fresh." Abu Sneida gazed at the setting sun and without uttering a single word, turned around, untied the rope and pushed the felucca back into the sea. I stood up, surprised, even angry. The boat rocked under my feet. It was the end of a day of work: time to rest, especially for him, at his age—at our age. I begged him to stop. Abu Sneida nodded with understanding and tied the felucca to the big boat once more. His son offered me a ladder. But then, right before I embarked, I turned back. I knew that the good things always happen when you're tired and no longer want to or feel able to continue. I stayed with Abu Sneida on his felucca. Two young fishermen of his tribe joined us from the yacht and together we sailed to the reef, away from the divers' boats.

When we arrived, Abu Sneida cast his net in a broad movement of his arm. He knows the cycles of the day and night, the changing of the seasons, the migratory roots of the fish—and he knows exactly where to aim. For more than fifty-five years Abu Sneida has been drifting on these waters, judiciously navigating his felucca between shallow, shark-sharp shoals, as if scanning sonar images of the bottoms etched in his brain by generations of fishermen before him.

Far away from Abu Sneida's Red Sea, traditional fishing cultures are disappearing across the globe. In the Miskito Cays, a duritara on its way to the "sleeping rocks"—turtle fishing grounds.

I wanted to jump in after the net to snap some photos. It was my favorite time of day: changeover time. Abu Sneida tried to hold me back, but I went into the water with my camera, shouting, "A photographer needs to photograph!" He gave up; he understood.

At first, it was difficult for me to notice the thin nylon strings that made up the net. I enjoyed this momentary blindness until the dissonance hit me: I no longer knew what exactly it was that I was trying to capture. Was it traditional fishing? The memory of beauty? Or the end of both?

I could see the boat's black shade above me, rocking in the veil of light that caresses the surface of the water at sunset. Abu Sneida was sitting up there, sharing stories with his younger companions as if forty years or more did not separate them. They must have been rapt with attention. Young Bedouins have great respect for their elders, their lore, and for the heritage of fishermen. However, if I should ask them about the future of fishing, they would probably squirm with unease. They would not give up on the good life reflected in the glamour of the tourist and diving boats constantly crossing the bay. Abu Sneida would listen to them, and his fixed broad smile would gradually fade: He knows he's the last fisherman.

I thought about today's sea, about the likes of Abu Sneida and traditional fishing. It is a deceptively simple world—hunters, hunting weapons, a voyage in a wild environment, the catch. But the idea that I, observing from a safe distance, was perhaps touching the last true hunters on Earth turned my own experience into an encounter with something primordial that was at the root of my soul, something arcane I had long ago lost.

Although I tend to call fishermen by their first names like the old friends they are, I was always a guest on their boats; I was an alien. I do not speak the languages they all understand. The language of *movements,* for example, spoken by their legs that absorb the boat's rocking motions with a gentle flex of the knee, by their hands so skilled in finding hidden gripping points around the deck as they dance in the storm over piles of gear and ropes. Nor do I speak the language of *gestures,* the automatic glimpses at the flag indicating the force of the gale, the looks to the horizon that help maintain orientation, the ears turned to prayers issuing from the boat's loudspeaker, the endless cycles of spitting salt that gets everywhere under their skin. And, of course, I do not speak the language of *action*—fishing.

In these special languages, you can read the ocean's surface ripples flickering in the light of the moon and the maneuvers of a school of fish scurrying along. Their lexicons can decipher the changing sounds of the wind; can predict the rise of tiny creatures from deep inside the ocean, and their inevitable fall between the jaws of its giant predators.

The *jangadeiros* in Brazil used to sail tens of kilometers far from the coast on their jangadas, spending up to several days on the high sea with no navigation devices.

All fishermen have to learn these languages, and every one of them has become fluent. They all know how to anticipate the movements and behaviors of fish, to move with staccato steps between piles of equipment and fellow fishermen, to navigate using state-of-the-art GPS instruments, to hang bait on hooks, to clean the deck, cook a meal, and even play cards. These are the languages of the fishing civilization, which transcend time, oceans, and boundaries.

Increasingly, my trips into these hunting grounds had become trips into the future: sped-up journeys where the image of the ocean was transformed as we traveled through uncharted waters. In this ocean, mighty "sharks" prey on schools of fish with satellite vision, mercilessly tracking them without fail; they cast their nets from horizon to far-flung horizon, swallowing more fish than Abu Sneida and all his forefathers put together could even imagine. In these ultra-modern waters there is no room anymore for the independent fisherman and his ancestral lore. Multiple stakeholders both local and foreign meddle in them, pouring capital and advanced technologies into them, paving new routes to distant markets. Increasingly, the fishing world is also growing accustomed to new terminology: sustainability, sustainable development, ecosystems, biodiversity, globalization—more and more words that sound utterly foreign to fishermen faced with the fewer and fewer fish in their good old seas.

I climbed back to the boat. Abu Sneida sorted his catch into a plastic crate. He threw in only those fish he could sell to the hotels and yachts anchored at the beach. All the rest—small, colorful, weird-looking and weird-tasting—he threw back to the sea. Let others eat them. Now he returned to the yacht, to his son. He threw a rope and tied the felucca to the fancy diving boat. On the felucca's floor, he hid a turtle he had caught; he knew that for whatever reason, tourists have a soft spot for these creatures and would never dare eat one—but he would. He then took out the bucket full of the few chosen fish and handed it over to his son.

At last, as the day drew to a final close, Abu Sneida climbed on the big boat and sat in the stern. I climbed after him. Now I, too, felt the weight of the years; perhaps my back would also bend as a result of all that condensed air I have inhaled in the deep. I took out a camera—digital this time, as even my insistence on using only film has been affected by the years. Two sunsets were reflected before me—his and mine—over the flat ocean of time. My camera can remember all the sunsets I have witnessed in a lifetime. I shot, and Abu Sneida smiled. "A fisherman," he nodded to himself. "A fisherman must fish."

Out of nowhere, a fishing thread appeared in the palm of his hand, bait as well, which he placed with extreme care on the hook. By the time his tea was respectfully served, the chord was in the water and his fingers plucked a gentle melody no fish could resist.

FURTHER READING AND RESOURCES

BOOKS

Fiction

Amado, Jorge. *Sea of Death*. New York: Avon Books, 1984.

Benchley, Peter. *The Girl of the Sea of Cortez*. Garden City, New York: Doubleday, 1982.

Hemingway, Ernest. *The Old Man and the Sea*. New York: Scribner, 1952.

Nonfiction

Earle, Sylvia. *Sea Change: A Message of the Oceans*. New York: G. P. Putnam's Sons, 1995.

Eyles, Carlos. *The Last of the Blue Water Hunters*. New York: Aqua Quest Publications, 2005.

Greenburg, Paul. *Four Fish*. New York: Penguin, 2010.

Greenlaw, Linda. *All Fishermen Are Liars: True Tales from the Dry Dock Bar*. New York: Hyperion, 2004.

Junger, Sebastian. *The Perfect Storm*. New York: W. W. Norton, 1997.

Kurlansky, Mark. *Cod: A Biography of the Fish that Changed the World*. New York: Walker, 1997.

———. *The Last Fish Tale: The Fate of the Atlantic and Survival in Gloucester, America's Oldest Fishing Port and Most Original Town*. New York: Ballantine, 2008.

Roberts, Callum. *The Unnatural History of the Sea*. Washington, D.C.: Island Press/Shearwater Books, 2007.

Safina, Carl. *Song for the Blue Ocean: Encounters Along the World's Coasts and Beneath the Seas*. New York: Henry Holt, 1998.

———. *The View from Lazy Point: A Natural Year in an Unnatural World*. New York: Henry Holt, 2010.

ORGANIZATIONS AND OTHER WEBSITES

Marine Environment

Australian Institute of Marine Science, http://aims.gov.au/

Center for Biological Diversity, http://www.biologicaldiversity.org/programs/oceans/

Center for Marine Biodiversity, http://www.marinebiodiversity.ca/

Coral Reef Alliance, http://coral.org/

Gulf of Maine Research Institute, http://www.gmri.org/

Reefkeeping magazine, http://www.reefkeeping.com/

ReefQuest Centre for Shark Research, http://www.elasmo-research.org/

Fishing and Conservation

Census of Marine Life, http://www.coml.org/

Food and Agriculture Organization of the United Nations, Fisheries and Aquaculture Department, http://www.fao.org/fishery/en

———, Small-scale Fisheries, http://www.fao.org/fishery/ssf/world/en

International Collective in Support of Fishworkers, http://www.icsf.net/

Marine Stewardship Council: Certified Sustainable Seafood, http://www.msc.org/

Natural Resources Defense Council, http://www.nrdc.org/issues/

Ocean Health Index, http://www.oceanhealthindex.org/

The Nature Conservancy, http://www.nature.org/how-we-work/index.htm?intc=nature.tnav.how

U.S. National Oceanic and Atmospheric Administration, http://www.noaa.gov/fisheries.html

Wildlife Conservation Society, http://www.wcs.org/

WWF (World Wildlife Fund), Marine Programme, http://wwf.panda.org/what_we_do/how_we_work/conservation/marine/

ACKNOWLEDGMENTS

This book has been written over a span of more than forty years—in practice and in spirit. Some of the stories happened to both of us; some happened to me and were told to Yair. Thus, registered and caught in the web of memory, both my and Yair's emotions and insights became part of those stories—as if we were together in the heart of the scenes.

Yair and I would like to extend our warmest thanks to publisher Bob Abrams and senior editor Joan Strasbaugh for their vision and unwavering support in making our dream come true: to combine the underwater and the fishing chapters of my life into a story with a compelling message. Many thanks to Carrie Bebris for her editorial magic and to Patricia Fabricant for her keen eye and beautiful design.

Special thanks to the people who volunteered their time and talent: Melanie Daniel for her steadfast commitment and wisdom in crystallizing the text; Omri Harel for his patience and his exhaustive research; Robert Daniel for his clarity and sound advice.

Also, we would like to thank Stephanie Keep, whose editorial acumen guided us throughout the writing of this book; Ami Asher for his help in shaping the voice of the text; Annaliese Jakimedes, Sebastian Troëng, Paul Maulineaux and G. Lazzaro Danzuso for their observations and writing; Wayne Bruzek for his magical performance with the images. And last, Asher Gal, my special friend and safety diver who many times pulled me out of the abyss—literally. Without his help many of the photographs seen here would not exist, and neither would I.

—Jeff Rotman

Mobarak Hemid Sobeih Mobarak "Umbi," *left*, captain of my diving boat in the Red Sea, stayed awake during my night dive when I drifted away and had already given up. Knowing the currents like the deep crevices of the palm of his hand, he was there for me in no time—as he has been for more than forty years.

Abd El Salam Mobarak Ibrahim "Abu Sneida," *right*, the ageless fisherman, blew his spiritual wind into my sails, and made me love and appreciate true men of the sea.

This book would not have been possible without them.

INDEX